ALCOHOL
AND THE
WRITER

BY DONALD W. GOODWIN

Is Alcoholism Hereditary? (second edition)

Anxiety

Psychiatric Diagnosis (fourth edition)
Co-authored with S.B. Guze

Phobia: The Facts

Longitudinal Research in Alcoholism
Co-authored with K.T. Van Dusen and S.A. Mednick

Alcoholism: The Facts

Alcoholism and Affective Disorders
Co-edited with Carlton Erickson

ALCOHOL AND THE WRITER

Donald W. Goodwin, M.D.

Andrews and McMeel
A Universal Press Syndicate Company
Kansas City • New York

C. 1

Library of Congress Cataloging-in-Publication Data

Goodwin, Donald W.
   Alcohol and the writer.

   Bibliography: p.
   1. Authors, American—Alcohol use. 2. Authors,
American—Psychology. 3. Alcoholism—United States.
4. Drinking customs—United States. 5. Authorship—
Psychological aspects. 6. Creative writing—
Psychological aspects. 7. Authors—Alcohol use.
8. Authors, American—Biography. I. Title.
PS129.G66   1988   810'.9'353   88-8161
ISBN 0-8362-5925-4

To Sarah
(both of them),
**William and Mary
and Caitlin**

Contents

Preface

I discovered books and alcohol at about the same age: seven. A boy's adventure book was lent to me by a neighbor, and I was hooked. Alcohol I owe to Uncle Ralph. He brought back his fiancée, Alice, to our home in Kansas to be married. He also brought a six-pack of beer. It was the first time alcohol had been permitted in the house. My father even refused beer advertising in his small-town newspaper. Ralph was a former football star, my boyhood hero. Alice was beautiful. Sports, girls, and the six-pack all became identified in my mind. They still are.

I was an English major in a small Methodist college where drinking was forbidden. Not wanting to get caught, the undergraduates drank a lot quickly. Certain books also were forbidden and it wasn't until I was a graduate student at Columbia University that I got my hands on *Lady Chatterley's Lover*. By this time I had decided that if it were forbidden, it must be fun.

While in New York I got a job writing feature columns for a newspaper syndicate. I discovered the three-martini lunch, but something was missing: the drinks were legal.

Supported by my columns, I went to medical school. I became a psychiatrist. I wanted to do research and needed something to study. I chose alcohol. There were sound reasons for doing so but one reason, I suspect, was Uncle Ralph and his six-pack.

As a researcher, my first discovery was that writers

drank a lot—maybe more than anyone else. Six Americans had won the Nobel Prize in literature and four were alcoholic. (A fifth drank heavily and the sixth was Pearl Buck, who probably didn't deserve the prize.) This was the highest alcoholism rate in any group I had ever encountered, higher even than the rate among Irish immigrants to Boston.

I wrote about my discovery in journals and magazines and received an offer to do a book on the subject, an offer I turned down. I continued doing research and eventually wrote books on alcohol and other subjects, such as anxiety and psychiatric illness, published by Oxford University Press and Random House. In 1988 I had a book published by Ballantine on alcoholism and heredity, a subject I have been studying for twenty years (mostly in Denmark).

Now, finally, I have written the long-postponed book about drinking writers. Through the years I have become more and more convinced that alcoholism among writers—American writers—constitutes an epidemic. The basis for the epidemic, illustrated by the tragic lives of some of its victims, is the subject of the book.

Acknowledgments

I want to thank my wife, Sally, for her usual indispensable help.

I want to thank Peter L. Simpson, friend, poet, and critic, for his help.

I want to thank another friend, George Wedge, for his help. Professor Wedge has a class on drinking writers at the University of Kansas and probably knows more about the subject than anyone else.

I want to thank Mrs. Evelyne Karson, whose patience and word processor are gifts from heaven.

I want to thank Gilman Ostrander, professor of history at the University of Waterloo in Ontario, for sharing with me one of the few viable theories—perhaps the only one—about why drinking writers drink.

Some of the material on Fitzgerald, O'Neill, and Simenon originally appeared in the *Journal of the American Medical Association*.

Grateful acknowledgment is made to the following for permission to quote their material:

Douglas Day, *Malcolm Lowry: A Biography,* copyright 1973 by Oxford University Press. Reprinted by permission of the publisher. Excerpts from the correspondence of Mrs. Malcolm Lowry which originally appeared in the Douglas Day biography reprinted by permission of Sterling Lord Literistic, Inc.

Canadian Literature, where Art Hill's article on Malcolm Lowry first appeared in the Autumn of 1974.

ALCOHOL
AND THE
WRITER

Introduction

Writing upon Drinking is in one respect, I think, like Drinking itself: one goes on imperceptibly, without knowing where to stop.

James Boswell, *London Magazine*

Can you name five American writers since Poe who did not die of alcoholism?

Sinclair Lewis

This book has a hypothesis. The hypothesis is that well-known writers in America during the first half of the twentieth century were extraordinarily susceptible to the disease called alcoholism.

It proposes, indeed, that alcoholism among American writers has been of epidemic dimensions. The evidence for this proposal will be presented.

As with many epidemics, however, this one has its detractors. The British writer Alistair Cooke, for example, said, "Hard drinking is a disease which afflicts every trade or profession. It has no more connection with writing than with plumbing."

But then (contradicting himself?) he says: "The Hemingway–Fitzgerald–Faulkner–O'Hara–O'Neill syndrome seems to be an American affliction which I don't understand." Add enough names to the syndrome and one presumably has an epidemic.

Michael Crichton is another doubter:

Even if it's true that authors drink more than other people, I doubt that they drink more than other people in what you might call "self-revealing occupations." I know a great many painters, famous and obscure, who drink to spectacular excess, and there is

1

certainly no scarcity of alcoholic actors and directors. What all these people share in common is a form of work which requires considerable public exposure—or the hope of it, or the threat of it. . . . I have been surprised to see how many people in "the arts" . . . are heavy drinkers, and for that matter how many do not drink at all, in that careful, somewhat embarrassed manner which indicates a drinking problem somewhere in the past.

Barnaby Conrad is also dubious. The public, he says, sees most working people while they are *working*—"the butcher, the baker, the doctor, the lawyer are at work when seen. The visible writer is off duty when seen." Off duty the writer is most likely relaxing, perhaps drinking, which perpetuates the drinking-writer myth. The public never sees him when he is home, sober, hunched over his typewriter. Conrad says, "Each year some 100,000 Americans die of alcoholism. They are not *all* writers."

Perhaps. Objective data are hard to come by. Death from cirrhosis of the liver, a disease closely associated with alcoholism, is documented by official statistics (official but always suspect). After bartenders, writers die of cirrhosis of the liver more than any other group (postmen least).

Those are the hard data. After that we come to polls.

Ring Lardner, Jr., obtained from an almanac a list of 187 twentieth-century American writers. One-third, to the best of his knowledge, were alcoholic, and he said he probably missed some. The rate, he guessed, was at least three times higher than the rate of alcoholism in the general population. (Lardner didn't really know the rate in the general population. Nobody knows. It depends on the definition of alcoholism. Household surveys cannot be depended upon, because the alcoholics are rarely home when the interviewer knocks on the door and many who are home probably lie.)

But a *third* of any group has to be high.

In the case of American writers who have won the Nobel Prize in literature, the alcoholism rate is over 70 percent.

First there was Sinclair Lewis—very alcoholic. Then came Eugene O'Neill—very alcoholic. Next was Pearl Buck, who hardly drank. (Women are less often alcoholic than men—protected, so to speak—and Buck was raised by missionary parents in China; hence, very protected.) Then followed William Faulkner—very alcoholic. Then Ernest Hemingway—alcoholic ("Drinking is a way of ending the day"). John Steinbeck comes next—a "two-fisted" drinker by some accounts, alcoholic by others. (Steinbeck's drinking is subjected to "scientific" scrutiny in chapter four—as scientific, anyway, as Freud's analysis of a lawyer based purely on a book about the man—and Steinbeck was found to be "alcoholic" also.)

Then we come to a Jewish laureate, Saul Bellow. Jews, like women, are "protected" against alcoholism, regardless of occupation, for reasons one can only guess at. Bellow drinks moderately.

These are the American laureates in literature, excluding T.S. Eliot, who spent most of his life in England, became a naturalized English citizen, and is usually not included in lists of American writers (especially if you are trying to prove something).*

The Polish writer Isaac Bashevis Singer won the award and lives in America, but writes in Yiddish—clear grounds for exclusion.

The 1987 Nobel Prize went to the Russian poet Joseph Brodsky, who was exiled fifteen years ago and became an American citizen. Most of his poems are in Russian. His drinking habits? When he heard the news about the prize, he was "sipping whiskey" at a lunch with John le Carré. The whiskey is mentioned in almost all the stories, reporters always being alert to the drinking-writing connection, but there is no record of Brodsky's being alcoholic. Alcoholism among Russian writers seems uncommon, despite the country's reputation for guzzling.

So that leaves seven laureates who fit the definition of American writer: four clearly alcoholic, the fifth probably alcoholic, the sixth a woman, and the seventh Jewish. Five of seven is 71 percent, surely the highest rate of alcoholism in any precisely defined group known to exist.

Another poll: Upton Sinclair, in the fifties, made a list of the fifteen worst drunks he had ever met. Ten were writers. Of the five others, all had done *some* writing. The study was unscientific, based on celebrities Sinclair had known.

One final piece of evidence: Nancy Andreasen, studying writers at the Writer's Workshop at the University of Iowa, found that 30

---

*Eliot may have been more of a drinker than many thought, according to a recent biography by Peter Ackroyd. "Throughout his life," Ackroyd reports, "he drank a good deal" and confessed that he "needed alcohol to get himself into the mood to write." In 14 B.C. Horace wrote, "No poems can please for long or live that are written by water-drinkers." Eliot's poems have lived long and perhaps we now know the reason. He was not, however, alcoholic by anybody's definition.

percent were alcoholic, using current criteria. More about this important study in the final chapter.

Perhaps the best way to convince a person that an epidemic existed is to have him write down in thirty minutes every American writer he can think of who was considered alcoholic by contemporaries or biographers or who drank enough to get the reputation of being alcoholic (perhaps, sometimes, unfairly). Here is such a list, restricted to writers who are dead (*safely* dead, I might add):

Edgar Allan Poe, Edwin Arlington Robinson, Ambrose Bierce, Theodore Dreiser, Hart Crane, Sinclair Lewis, Eugene O'Neill, Edna St. Vincent Millay, Dorothy Parker, F. Scott Fitzgerald, Ring Lardner, Ernest Hemingway, John O'Hara, William Faulkner, John Steinbeck, Dashiell Hammett, Thomas Wolfe, John Berryman, J.P. Marquand, Wallace Stevens, E.E. Cummings, Theodore Roethke, Edmund Wilson, James Thurber, Jack London, Tennessee Williams, Truman Capote, William Inge, Robert Benchley, Jack Kerouac, O. Henry (William Sydney Porter), Mr. Dooley (Finley Peter Dunne), John Cheever, Conrad Aiken, Woolcott Gibbs, Stephen Crane, Philip Barry, James Jones, Robert Ruark, William Saroyan, Irwin Shaw, Delmore Schwartz, Robert Lowell, Randall Jarrell, Jean Stafford, James Agee, Ralph Maloney, Raymond Chandler, and, according to its nonalcoholic drama critic Brendan Gill, almost every writer for the *New Yorker* during the thirties.

Only one, Poe, was nineteenth century. The others all died in the twentieth. The list is not complete. Professor George Wedge at the University of Kansas, probably the world's leading authority on drinking writers, has compiled a list of 150 famous American writers who were alcoholic or very heavy drinkers. My list was off the top of the head and took thirty minutes. Easy.

What is hard is to think of *non*alcoholics among American writers of the twentieth century. After you've mentioned Robert Frost, Edith Wharton, Willa Cather, Upton Sinclair, Edgar Guest, Pearl Buck, Herman Wouk, James Michener, Jessamyn West, and a few others, whom have you? There are others, of course, but most are more recent writers, still too young to have biographies of them.

One of the cravings occasioned by alcohol is that of defining the term *alcoholism*. The word is used liberally in this book. What does it mean?

Charles Jackson said that an alcoholic was a person who could take it or leave it, so he took it, but most people crave a better definition. The chapter on Steinbeck examines the definition of alcoholism in some detail. Let us say it embraces a compulsion to drink sufficiently strong so that it interferes with a person's health, social relations, and productivity.

The problem in diagnosis is not with the unequivocal alcoholics like O'Neill, Faulkner, and Lowry, but with drinkers who, like Hemingway and Steinbeck, go out of their way to deny a personal problem with alcohol. Diagnosis is further complicated in that friends and relatives of a writer of the latter class see him at different times drinking more or less than at other times (and friends and relatives are not always reliable, either).

For example, Steinbeck's biographer wrote more than eleven hundred pages about his subject and never once referred to numerous reports that Steinbeck was continually drunk during his tour in North Africa as a war correspondent. Hemingway's drinking habits have been the source of many discrepancies. According to some observers—and himself—he leaped out of bed at 6 A.M., wrote religiously until noon, producing about five hundred words, and never drank before noon. According to his son, Gregory, he arose at 5 A.M. and wrote till 10. "I knew he was a writer, but I never saw him writing . . . since I always got up around ten. By that time he would be standing around with a drink in his hand, saying, 'What do you want to do today?' . . . he would drink all day and all night long, yet get up and write the next morning."

Small differences, but whom to believe? Perhaps Ernest was referring to one period in his life and Gregory to another. One has to examine the total picture and make a judgment, which still may be fallacious.

On one point there appears to be unanimous agreement: American writers were heavy into alcohol during the first half of the twentieth century. It was the talk of the literary world.

"I think you have to look awfully hard in twentieth century

American literature to find a great writer who was not a drunk, or a serious, consistent drinker," writes Matthew J. Bruccoli.

"Booze has played as big a role in the lives of modern American writers as talent, money, and women," writes Alfred Kazin.

"In this country more than any other that I know of," writes Brendan Gill, "the relationship between writers and alcohol is a curiously close one."

Responding to Alistair Cooke's charge that writers drink no more than plumbers, Barnaby Conrad observed that if the percentage of great plumbers who drink was as high as the percentage of great writers who drink, the "drains of America would be constantly clogged."

Conrad had an author friend who was wont to hold up his glass, "steel blue with straight gin, brandish it as though it were the ultimate prerequisite to fine writing, and declare defensively, 'Name me an American writer who wasn't a drunk except Mary Baker Eddy!'" Another author friend pointed to the bottle of Scotch on the table between Conrad and himself and remarked thoughtfully, "What is there about a full bottle of booze that makes every American writer feel constrained to drain it as soon as possible?"

Every working writer and English major has a store of drinking-writer jokes. My favorite:

> Dorothy Parker and a friend went to a funeral home in New York to pay their last respects to a famous writer who had just died an untimely death.
>
> The friend sighed as they gazed down into the coffin, "Doesn't he look just wonderful?"
>
> "And why shouldn't he?" Dorothy replied. "He hasn't had a drink in three days."

The epidemic existed all right. It was real.

How to explain the high rate of alcoholism among authors? Is the association purely chance? Do writers drink because of the nature of their work or the life they lead? Do bad or obscure writers become alcoholic as often as famous writers? (Perhaps fame itself leads to alcoholism.) Do writing ability and alcoholism perhaps have common roots? Is there some characteristic of a good writer, something innate, that predisposes him to alcoholism?

The writers in this book were chosen to shed light on these questions. Six are American; four were Nobel laureates. The seventh is a Belgian novelist who lived in France and drank like the French and then moved to America and drank like the Americans. The eighth is an English novelist whose cure for alcoholism—not entirely successful—was to live in the Canadian wilderness.

The choices were deliberate: an attempt to view a complex problem from many angles. The final chapter attempts to explain why it all happened.

F. Scott Fitzgerald, novelist, short story writer and scenarist, died at his Hollywood home yesterday. His age was 44. He suffered a heart attack three weeks ago.

Mr. Fitzgerald and his life and writings epitomized "all the sad young men" of the post-war generation. With the skill of a reporter and ability of an artist he captured the essence of a period when flappers and gin and "the beautiful and the damned" were the symbols of the carefree madness of an age.

Roughly, his own career began and ended with the Nineteen Twenties.

In 1940 this was the way it seemed. Fitzgerald was "the historian of the Jazz Age" and a writer of talent, but sold out to Hollywood and the *Saturday Evening Post,* and died in obscurity, a has-been. The obituary ends with Fitzgerald's own comparison of himself to a "cracked plate."

He wrote in *Esquire* a few years earlier:

Sometimes, though, the cracked plate has to be retained in the pantry, has to be kept in service as a household necessity. It can never be warmed on the stove nor shuffled with the other plates in the dishpan; it will not be brought out for company but it will do to hold crackers late at night or go into the ice-box with the left overs.

Fitzgerald seemed a leftover, all right. His last royalty statement from Scribner's showed sales of forty copies (including seven copies of *The Great Gatsby*) for a royalty of $13.13. Matthew J. Bruccoli, a leading Fitzgerald scholar and source of these figures, provides some other figures a few pages later in his 1981 biography:

In the forty years since Fitzgerald's death, Scribner's has sold at least eight million copies of his books. Twenty-one new volumes of his writings have been published, along with some fifty biographical and critical books and pamphlets. His work has been translated into thirty-five languages. *The Great Gatsby* has become a classroom staple and sells some 300,000 copies a year in the United States.

F. Scott Fitzgerald is now permanently placed with the greatest writers who ever lived, where he wanted to be all along. Where he belongs.

The biographies are still coming out, almost yearly, it seems: Scott Donaldson's *Fool for Love: F. Scott Fitzgerald* in 1983, a translation of André Le Vot's fine French biography in the same year; and in 1984 another full-scale biography, this one by James R. Mellow, called *Invented Lives: F. Scott and Zelda Fitzgerald.*

Fitzgerald, in short, has become a literary property. The same thing happened to Poe after he died at forty: one biography after another, continuing to the present day. Poe and Fitzgerald had several things in common. Both died young and were considered "failed writers" when they died. Both wrote mainly to eke out an income; their best work consists of only a small fraction of their total output. Both were severely alcoholic and probably died as a result of their disease.

Both, at their best, were marvelous writers, but their personal tragedies, in the public mind, have become so blended with their artistic achievements that it is almost impossible to separate them.

With Poe there is uncertainty about the simple facts of his life. At least the *facts* about Fitzgerald are known; the reasons are the hard thing to come by.

F. Scott Fitzgerald was born in 1896 in St. Paul, where he spent most of his boyhood. His father was a business failure but the family lived comfortably on an inheritance from Scott's maternal grandfather. Scott attended a Roman Catholic boarding school and then went to Princeton but dropped out of college in his junior year because of illness and poor grades. The following year he reentered Princeton, but after two months joined the army as a second lieutenant. In this period he began working on his first novel, *This Side of Paradise*, finishing a first draft at Princeton and a second draft at Fort Leavenworth, where he took officer's training. He wanted to go overseas—it was 1918—but instead was stationed near Montgomery, Alabama. There he met his future wife, Zelda Sayre, at a country-club dance.

After the war Fitzgerald worked for a time in New York for an advertising agency, then returned to St. Paul where he finished his novel. It was published by Charles Scribner's Sons and became a bestseller. A celebrity at twenty-four, Fitzgerald married Zelda and began writing a second novel, *The Beautiful and Damned,* as well as stories for the *Saturday Evening Post.*

The Fitzgeralds spent much of the 1920s in Europe, living in Paris and on the French Riviera. His third novel, *The Great Gatsby,* was published in 1925. It sold rather poorly, but Fitzgerald made a good income from short stories and he and Zelda lived on a lavish scale. Fitzgerald was well regarded by other writers, especially after *The Great Gatsby,* and he remained a minor celebrity during the 1920s.

As the 1920s faded, so did Fitzgerald. In the 1930s he published one more novel, *Tender Is the Night,* and a number of stories, but his literary production fell off and with it his income and fame. His wife became psychotic—Oscar Forel in Switzerland diagnosed her condition as schizophrenic—and was hospitalized for much of the rest of her life. She died in 1947.

Fitzgerald lived for a time near Baltimore while she was being treated by Adolph Meyer, then, in 1937, moved to Hollywood to write for the movies. There he met the columnist Sheilah Graham, who years later wrote a book about being his mistress. He disliked writing for the movies and had little success at it (he received only one screen credit). He was working on a novel, *The Last Tycoon,* when, in 1940, at age forty-four, he died of a heart attack in Hollywood. His death was little noted. Many people thought he had died years before. Others thought "F. Scott Fitzgerald" was a character from a novel of the 1920s. When he died, few of his books were in print.

Then a curious thing happened. Starting in the early 1950s, Fitzgerald became popular again. His books are all in print now and read by millions. *The Great Gatsby* has become a classic, required reading for English majors everywhere, and hardly a month goes by without the mention of Scott or Zelda in a magazine or newspaper. How would Fitzgerald have taken all this? His friends agree he would have loved it.

But not all of it perhaps. As Leslie Fiedler has pointed out, there is a tradition in Western literature that great writers should have a flaw, a "charismatic weakness." Fitzgerald was a drunk and this may have accounted for his fame—if Fiedler is right—as much as has his literary achievement.

Fitzgerald's drunkenness, his charismatic flaw, is extraordinarily well documented. It is described in detail in his biographies, Fitzgerald discusses it in letters and essays, and his novels and stories are crowded with drunkards who bear a strong resemblance to their creator.

When did Fitzgerald become alcoholic? There are suggestions that drunkenness had a special attraction for him long before he took his first drink. As a boy he enjoyed *pretending* to be drunk. According to one biographer, he made such a plausible drunk that girls told their mothers he had been drinking and he "reveled in his reputation as roué." Fitzgerald had his first drink at sixteen. He shocked a friend by tossing down several Bronx cocktails and then to amuse passersby, pretended he was the friend's father. From the beginning exhibitionism and drinking were inseparable for F. Scott Fitzgerald.

At Princeton he acquired a reputation for being unable to hold his liquor, even though he generally drank in moderation. He may have had little choice. "It was still an era when parents promised their sons gold watches if they abstained till they were 21," wrote Andrew Turnbull. "Alcohol in any form was forbidden on campus, and conspicuous drunks were frowned upon, so Fitzgerald, like most of his contemporaries, confined himself to beer in the saloons along Nassau Street."

How much Fitzgerald really drank at Princeton is uncertain, because he bragged so much about whatever drinking he did do. "Pardon me if my hand is shaky," he wrote his girlfriend, "but I just had a quart of sauterne and 3 Bronxes." Boasting about drinking became habitual, so that years later he would introduce himself as "F. Scott Fitzgerald, the well-known alcoholic." In college he liked to appear more drunk than he was—after one beer his knees sagged and he went into his drunk act—and this too persisted into later life. In Paris Hemingway used to be greatly irritated when Fitzgerald pretended to pass out after a few drinks.

No doubt this contributed to observations about Fitzgerald's "intolerance" for alcohol, which was probably a myth but which is still repeated in even the best biographies. That Fitzgerald became drunk on small amounts of alcohol is contradicted by numerous accounts of steady consumption of very unsmall amounts. Poe had the same reputation and probably for the same reason: histrionics become part of the drinker's arsenal of tricks for disarming potential critics. Also, the true alcoholic never does all of his drinking where people can see it; the "invisible" drinks must be counted into the total.

Another probable myth about Fitzgerald was that he drank because he had low blood sugar (hypoglycemia). Bruccoli had access to Fitzgerald's medical records and says there was no evidence that he had hypoglycemia. He did sometimes have ice cream for breakfast, but this may have been to relieve hangover heartburn. (Alcohol will *cause* hypoglycemia, but only in individuals in a state of semistarvation.)

Allowing, however, for his histrionics, there seems no question that by the time Fitzgerald was discharged from the army at age twenty-three and went to work in New York, he was getting drunk regularly and in earnest. He disliked writing slogans for the advertising agency. Zelda refused to marry him because he had too little money, and so he drank. "As I hovered ghost-like in the Plaza Red Room of a Saturday afternoon," he later recalled, "or went to lush and liquid parties in the East Sixties or tippled with Princetonians in the Biltmore Bar, I was haunted always by my other life—my drab room in the Bronx, my square foot on the subway. . . ."

Quitting his job, he went on a three-week bender—his first. Its description in *This Side of Paradise* is one of literature's most vivid descriptions of a binge. It ended on 1 July 1919, the day Prohibition began. Fitzgerald sobered up to finish his first novel, but now success, rather than disappointment and poverty, was the occasion for drinking. He became an extravagant as well as histrionic drunk, leaving lavish tips and stuffing $50 bills in his coat and vest pockets for all to see. He and Zelda made frequent spectacles of themselves—clowning at parties, leaping fully clothed into the Plaza fountain, rolling champagne bottles down Fifth Avenue at dawn. All of this received a great deal of publicity and the Fitzgerald legend had begun.

And so had the problems—the social, domestic, professional, and finally medical problems that, coming singly or in flurries, characterize the natural history of an alcoholic. Fitzgerald began losing friends ("Here come the Fitzgeralds," people would groan).

He was suspended from his college club for misbehavior at house parties. He got into brawls and was jailed. And as he and Zelda drank more, they fought more. Friends warned they were headed for catastrophe. One acquaintance, Malcolm Cowley, recorded in his diary:

> In the evening Zelda—drunk—having decided to leave Fitz and having nearly been killed walking down RR tracks, blew in. Fitz came shortly after. He had caught the same train with no money or ticket. They threatened to put him off but finally let him stay on—Zelda refusing to give him any money. They continued their fight. . . .

Zelda complained about Fitzgerald's drinking, once telling a friend, "Don't let drinking get you in the position it's gotten Scott if you want your marriage to be any good," but Hemingway and others believed she encouraged him to drink because it kept him from his work, of which she, having literary aspirations herself, was jealous. Sometimes, though, she defended her husband, as when (as related in a letter of Zelda's) she told her father that Fitzgerald when sober was the sweetest person in the world, to which her father replied, "He's never sober."

By Fitzgerald's midtwenties there was no question about his alcoholism; he recognized it and so did his friends. "I couldn't get sober long enough to be able to tolerate being sober," he wrote in a letter after one interminable party, and his benders became more frequent. "The year after their marriage," Turnbull writes, "their drinking around New York had been a gay, irresponsible, left-over-from-college affair, but now their fun was turning destructive. Fitzgerald vanished into the city on two- and three-day drunks, after which neighbors would find him asleep on his front lawn. At dinner parties, he crawled around under the table, or hacked off his tie with a kitchen knife, or tried to eat soup with a fork." Once he drove his car into a pond because it seemed more fun.

By his late twenties the fun was gone. "His drinking," Turnbull said, "was something he went off and did by himself, like taking a pill. It had no connection with anyone else." His work suffered and he felt guilty. When twenty-eight years old he wrote his editor about how he had "deteriorated" over the previous three years: "I produced exactly one play, half a dozen short stories and three or four articles—an average of about one hundred words a day. If I'd spent the time . . . staying healthy it'd be different, but I spent it uselessly . . . drinking and raising hell."

At this time he still wrote only when sober, but in his early thirties Fitzgerald began deliberately mixing liquor with his work. He was usually sorry afterward. Once he apologized to his editor for drinking so much when writing *Tender Is the Night*. "A short story," he explained, "can be written on a bottle, but for a novel you need the mental speed that enables you to keep the whole pattern in your head."

Fitzgerald's attempts to control his drinking were reminiscent of other alcoholics'. He often went on the wagon—toward the end of his life, with Sheilah Graham's help, he stayed dry for six months—but inevitably fell off. He tried eating candy. He kept a schedule of his drinks and tried rationing himself. For a time he limited himself to beer. Nothing worked, so in the end, as alcoholics will, he rationalized. Alcohol was a "writer's vice." It "heightened feeling." Once, surveying the debris from a New Year's Eve party, he commented, "Just think—it's like this now all over the country."

Then his health gave way. He first became hypochondriacal and developed insomnia. The doctors told him he should take more exercise and not drink. He took barbiturates and chloral hydrate to help him sleep, increasing the dosage through the years but never apparently to the point of addiction. In his midthirties Fitzgerald had episodes of spitting blood and twitching legs and was hospitalized. As a college student he had had a mild case of tuberculosis—so mild it may have been subclinical—and it is unclear whether the blood was gastric or pulmonary in origin. Fitzgerald worried about his health and had a collection of photographs, obtained from a temperance worker, showing the ill effects of alcohol on the kidneys and other organs. These pictures he mulled over and made jokes about. He hired nurses to help him stop drinking, but sneaked drinks when they were not looking.

Fitzgerald's benders in his last years are vividly described by Sheilah Graham, and by Budd Schulberg in his novel *The Disenchanted*. His personality had always undergone marked change when he drank, but now the change was spectacular. Fitzgerald, sober, was gentle, considerate, charming. On alcohol he became belligerent and maudlin. What passed for drunken clowning in his younger days was now pathetic and grotesque. Fitzgerald knew this, but felt powerless to change.

Zelda's psychiatrists, Adolph Meyer and Thomas Rennie, urged him to obtain psychiatric treatment, but he refused on the grounds that it might destroy his effectiveness as a writer and he cited several writers who he felt had suffered this fate. Fitzgerald was fatalistic about the outcome of his drinking. "All drunks," he said, "die between 38 and 48." At forty-four he had two heart attacks and died of the second.

Here end the facts, to the extent they are determinable, and the speculation begins. What kind of person was Fitzgerald? How did he become that person? What made him a good writer? What made him an alcoholic? In what way, if any, were his writing ability and alcoholism related?

Fitzgerald, everyone agrees, was complicated. J.B. Priestley detected in his "richly confused character" two opposing strains. There was the starry-eyed, romantic Fitzgerald, the perennial adolescent, spellbound by glamour and the glitter of life. Contrasting with this "hot, messy" Fitzgerald was the tough-minded Fitzgerald: cool, detached, ruthlessly honest about himself and the world he recorded. Malcolm Cowley noted the same "double vision"—the way Fitzgerald took part in the "ritual orgies" of his time but remained detached, standing "outside the ballroom, a little midwestern boy with his nose to the glass, wondering how much the tickets cost and who paid for the music."

Fitzgerald viewed himself as not one man, or two, but many. "There never was a good biography of a good novelist," he wrote to Hemingway. "There couldn't be. He's too many people if he's any good." Being many people could be unpleasant. "Life is much more successfully looked at from a single window," concludes a Fitzgerald character. Sometimes, Fitzgerald admitted, he had trouble deciding whether he was real or a character from one of his novels. Nevertheless, he was proud of his complexity. "The test of a first-rate intelligence," he wrote in *The Crack-Up,* "is the ability to hold two opposed ideas in the mind at one time and still retain the ability to function."

Fitzgerald's personality consisted not of one set of contradictions but of many. He had a very high opinion of himself, and a very low one. He was dreamy and gregarious. He adored the rich and despised them. He was a sensualist and a puritan. He loved fame but never quite believed in his own because it had come so suddenly. Even in his craft Fitzgerald was contradictory—he spelled abominably and yet achieved perhaps the best prose style of any American novelist of his generation.

He recognized the contradictions early. At fifteen Fitzgerald described himself as possessing a "sort of aristocratic egotism" based on "superior mentality." He thought there was nothing he could not do, "except, perhaps, become a mechanical genius." Among his assets he included good looks, charm, magnetism, poise, and the "ability to dominate others." He was particularly impressed by his "subtle fascination over women."

Having listed his assets, he named his liabilities.

I was rather worse than most boys, due to a latent unscrupulousness. . . . I was cold, capable of being cruel, lacked a sense of honor, and was mordantly selfish. . . . I had a curious cross section of weakness running through my character. . . . I was completely the slave of my own moods and often dropped into a surly sensitiveness most unprepossessing to others . . . at bottom I lacked the essentials . . . courage, perseverance or self-respect.

He was either up or down. "My inordinate vanity," he wrote, "was liable to be toppled over at one blow by an unpleasant remark or a missed tackle." Vanity was the warp of his personality, shame the woof.

Fitzgerald had a robust constitution but a delicate, fastidious nature. His father once said he would give $5 to hear Scott swear. As a boy, Fitzgerald was phobic about his feet—he was ashamed for them to be seen unshod and he avoided swimming parties and other occasions where this might happen. The smelly, seamy side of life always offended him. Writing about the "working classes" was a chore he rarely did well. Part of his attraction to the rich, apparently, was his conviction that the rich never sweat. Despite his reputation for hedonism, his attitudes toward sex were chaste and Victorian. His novels were romantic but obstinately unsexy—the opposite of today's fiction.

With this squeamishness went a feminine strain which Fitzgerald himself remarked on: "I'm half feminine—at least my mind is." Women told him that he understood women and he conceded that this was true. Most of his memorable characters were women, as was the narrator of his last novel. Fitzgerald was not effeminate, however, and so far as the record shows, was normally sexed.

What was the origin of these traits? To some extent his mother may have been responsible for his vanity and high expectations of himself. Her two other children died shortly before Scott was born, and she spoiled him inordinately. She dressed him in Eton caps and collars and urged him to excel in whatever he did. He was ashamed of her—she was homely and eccentric—and resented the way she coddled him. If his feeling of self-importance came from his mother, so, to a degree, did his sense of inferiority.

The latter also was a product of the family's financial circumstances. There was money, but not a lot; enough for dancing classes and prep school and Princeton, where Scott could meet the really wealthy and learn the social graces; but not enough to compete with the wealthy or banish the fear of poverty. When Fitzgerald was a boy and his father lost his job, Fitzgerald prayed, "Dear God, please don't let us go to the poorhouse," and never, even during the 1920s when he was prosperous, was the poorhouse far from his mind. Fitzgerald wanted more than anything else to be rich, for to be rich was to be loved and secure and, for most of his life, Fitzgerald felt neither.

Wealth, love, and security—they were all bound together and partly explain the conflict in Fitzgerald's professional goals, his desire to be a great writer, assured of love eternal, and at the same time a popular writer, meaning a wealthy writer. These mixed goals explain the unevenness of his work but not the trait that made both goals, on occasion, attainable, namely, his authentic writing talent.

A writing talent is a mysterious thing. Like musical ability, it appears to be partly innate and unlearned. Individuals can be trained to write, but only to a point; there is a ceiling to talent. Fitzgerald's ceiling was high indeed. His motivation to write—his desire for love and praise—may have been conditioned by experience, but his ability to write is harder to explain. It required a sensitivity to experience, an alertness to the "infinite possibilities of life," plus a verbal facility, qualities that are difficult to attribute solely to the circumstances of his upbringing.

Alcoholism also may involve heredity in that it seems to run in families and cannot be attributed purely to environmental factors in every instance. Fitzgerald's biographers report that his father and two maternal uncles "drank." How much they drank and whether they had problems from drinking are not known.

If writing talent and alcoholism are partly innate and somehow related, they may have a common meeting point in another disorder which appears to have a genetic aspect: manic-depressive disease. This illness also runs in families. Fitzgerald's enthusiasms at times bordered on hypomania but were never, it appears, frankly manic. He was often momentarily depressed, and in *The Crack-Up,* a series of articles written for *Esquire* in 1936, he describes three episodes of depression (one at Princeton, the other after the war, and the third current) that were prolonged and qualitatively different from anything he had known. The symptoms were classical, their description incomparable. "In the real dark night of the soul it is always three o'clock in the morning." Even their termination was typical of manic-depressive depression: "Unless madness or drugs or drink come into it," he wrote, the depression eventually comes to a "deadend" and is succeeded by a "vacuous quiet."

However, drink almost always came into it. In alcoholics it is often difficult to diagnose other disorders; heavy drinking both obliterates and mimics other syndromes. Fitzgerald was no exception to this.

To understand the association of alcoholism and writing talent it might be helpful to examine the pharmacological effect of alcohol on people and specifically on writers. This requires making assumptions about writing and alcohol that may miss the mark in individual cases. Here, nevertheless, are some points where writing and alcohol may interact or serve common ends.

Writing is a form of exhibitionism; alcohol lowers inhibitions and prompts exhibitionism in many people. Writing requires an interest in people; alcohol increases sociability and makes people more interesting. Writing involves fantasy; alcohol promotes fantasy. Writing requires self-confidence; alcohol bolsters confidence. Writing is lonely work; alcohol assuages loneliness. Writing demands intense concentration; alcohol relaxes.

This, of course, may explain why writers (and many other people) drink, but does not explain alcoholism. Fitzgerald knew why he drank: it brought him closer to people and relieved his tortured sensitivity. People meant more to Fitzgerald than anything else. He yearned to be close to them, intimate, involved. His shyness prevented it and so did his fear of rejection, of having his inadequacy exposed and his sense of importance shattered. Alcohol was a bridge. "I found," says an alcoholic in one of his stories, "that with a few drinks I got expansive and somehow had the ability to please people. . . . Then I began to take a whole lot of drinks to keep going and have everybody think I was wonderful."

Alcohol also reduced the "sensory overload" to which writers are prone. As a writer, Fitzgerald felt he had to register everything—all the emanations and nuances of the world around him, the "inexhaustible variety of life." Like many writers, he had difficulty turning off this "afferent" side of his talent. Careful writing consists of an endless chain of small decisions—choosing the best word, excluding this, including that—and the good writer, while writing, is an obsessional. Restricting obsessions to a nine-to-five workday is difficult; the wheels keep turning, and writers are notorious sufferers of insomnia. Alcohol, for a time, emancipates the writer from the tyranny of mind and memory.

Fitzgerald drank, as Baudelaire said of Edgar Allan Poe, "not as an epicure, but barbarously, with a speed and dispatch altogether American, as if he were performing a homicidal function, as if he had to kill something inside himself, a worm that would not die." The puzzling thing about Fitzgerald was not why he drank, but why he drank as Poe did. What was Fitzgerald's worm? What was he trying to kill? Nothing written by Fitzgerald or about him tells us. The origin of his alcoholism is as inscrutable as the mystery of his writing talent.

Bibliographical Note

The Fitzgerald revival was launched in 1951 with Arthur Mizener's excellent biography, *The Far Side of Paradise* (Boston: Houghton Mifflin). In 1962 another first-rate biography appeared, Andrew Turnbull's *Scott Fitzgerald* (New York: Charles Scribner's Sons). Other good biographies appeared over the next decade, but the definitive work on Fitzgerald was published in 1981: Matthew J. Bruccoli's *Some Sort of Epic Grandeur* (New York: Harcourt Brace Jovanovich). A Fitzgerald scholar for more than twenty years, Bruccoli conducted an exhaustive investigation of Fitzgerald's life and work, and his book shows it.

In 1984 another major biography appeared, *Invented Lives*, by James R. Mellow (Boston: Houghton Mifflin). As one critic said, *Invented Lives* is "readable, polished and professional, but Mr. Mellow has little new to add . . . the story is so good it seems to tell itself."

Fitzgerald's correspondence has been collected in the *Letters of F. Scott Fitzgerald*, edited by Andrew Turnbull (New York: Charles Scribner's Sons, 1963). Budd Schulberg and Sheilah Graham/ Gerold Frank have described Fitzgerald's later years in, respectively, *The Disenchanted* (New York: Random House, 1950) and *Beloved Infidel* (New York: Henry Holt & Co., 1958). Ernest Hemingway gives a savage account of Fitzgerald's drinking in *The Moveable Feast* (New York: Charles Scribner's Sons, 1964). Joan M. Allen tries in *Candles and Carnival Lights* (New York: New York University Press, 1978) to explain some of Fitzgerald's personality and work by his "Catholic sensibility," but not very convincingly.

3

HEMINGWAY
Scenes from New York
and Havana

How do you like it now, gentlemen?
Hemingway

Late in 1949, on their way to Europe, Ernest Hemingway and his wife, Mary, stopped in New York for a few days. Meeting them at the airport was Lillian Ross, a writer for the *New Yorker* who later wrote a profile on Hemingway. She had met Hemingway before, he liked her, and she spent the better part of two days with them in New York.

Getting off the airplane, Hemingway had his arm over the shoulder of a little man who was perspiring heavily. The little man had been his seat companion on the flight and Hemingway had insisted that he read the unfinished manuscript of his new book, *Across the River and into the Trees*. The little man attempted to escape from the embrace, but Hemingway held onto him affectionately. "He read book all way up on plane," Hemingway said. "He liked book, I think," beaming down at his friend. (Then, and throughout the visit, Hemingway spoke a kind of Indian talk, dropping the articles.)

The friend said, "Whew!"

"Book too much for him," Hemingway said. "Book starts slow, then increase in pace till it becomes impossible to stand. I bring emotion up to where you can't stand it, then we level off, so we won't have to provide oxygen tents for the readers. Book is like engine. We have to slack her off gradually."

In addition to the Indian talk, Hemingway often spoke in metaphors: airplane metaphors and particularly baseball and boxing metaphors. The combination is distinctive.

50

Hemingway finally released his seat companion, shook his hands, and thanked him for reading the book.

"Pleasure," the man said, and walked off unsteadily.

Hemingway's state of sobriety at the time was uncertain. Drinks, of course, are served on airplanes. Miss Ross prudently avoids the subject, but does give a memorable description of Hemingway's appearance.

> Hemingway had on a red plaid wool shirt, a figured woolen necktie, a tan wool sweater-vest, a brown tweed jacket tight across the back and with sleeves too short for his arms, gray flannel slacks, Argyle socks, and loafers, and he looked bearish, cordial, and constricted. His hair, which was very long in back, was gray, except at the temples, where it was white; his moustache was white, and he had a ragged, half-inch full white beard. There was a bump about the size of a walnut over his left eye. He had on steel rimmed spectacles, with a piece of paper under the nosepiece.

Hemingway was fifty years old. He lived on a farm in Cuba. He disliked New York. They had stopped only to do some shopping before boarding the *Ile de France* for Paris.

They had fourteen pieces of luggage. Hemingway was in no hurry to go into town. While a porter watched the luggage, Miss Ross and the Hemingways went into the airport bar. Hemingway ordered double bourbons and talked about the new book. "After you finish a book, you know, you are dead. But no one knows you are dead. All they see is the responsibility that comes in after the terrible responsibility of writing." For a welcome change, he dropped the Indian talk, but not the sports metaphors: "They can't yank novelists like they can pitchers," he said, referring to the rewriting he had to do.

Hemingway ordered another round of double bourbons and at least one more round before they left the bar. He turned down a cigarette, saying smoking ruined his sense of smell, which he needed to smell animals. He talked about how well he got along with animals. In Montana, he said, he once lived with a bear. The bear slept with him, got drunk with him, and was a close friend. This story sounds untrue but it is a matter of record that Hemingway did once, in a circus, carry on what appeared to be a lively conversation with a bear. People were always saying he looked like a bear and perhaps that helped.

In any case, Miss Ross and the Hemingways finally got a cab for Manhattan. Hemingway sat in front where he could keep his eyes carefully on the road, a habit he had acquired during World War I. Hemingway talked about what he would do in New York. He particularly wanted to see a prizefight. He said it was important to see several fights a year. "If you quit going for too long a time, then you never go near them," he said. "That would be very dangerous." Then he said something that was curious and perhaps revealing. "If you quit going to fights, finally you end up in one room and won't move."

Was Ernest Hemingway—a man constantly on the move, hunting, deep-sea fishing, watching bullfights, cockfights and prizefights, surrounding himself with people—was the famous, gregarious, daredevil Hemingway actually a victim of agoraphobia whose remedy was perpetual motion?

If you don't keep doing things you end up in one room and won't move: a revealing touch, one to be explored later.

Hemingway told other stories on the way into Manhattan. He told about a duck hunting trip on a cold night in Italy and the Chianti that kept him warm. A very high proportion of the stories that Hemingway told included mention of alcohol.

Checking into the Sherry-Netherland Hotel, Hemingway made two instant decisions: call the Kraut and order champagne.

The Kraut was Marlene Dietrich. Add to the Indian talk, the sports and aviational metaphors, and the references to booze, a fondness for nicknames. Hemingway, of course, was called Papa by everyone, including his wife. The nicknames for his three sons were Bumby, Mouse, and Gigi. He had nicknames for his four wives, Pickles being a favorite for his fourth. Like the Indian talk and the metaphors, it could get a little irritating.

The champagne arrived and Hemingway returned to a favorite subject—writing. On critics: "What the hell! If they can do you harm, let them do it. It is like being a third baseman and protesting because they hit line drives to you."

Moving on over to the pitcher's mound, when he was pitching, he said, he never struck anybody out, except under extreme necessity. "I knew I had only so many fast balls in that arm," he said. "Would make them pop to short instead, or fly out, or hit it on the ground, bouncing."

He compared himself to other writers: "I started out very quiet and I beat Mr. Turgenev. Then I trained hard and I beat Mr. de Maupassant. I fought two draws with Mr. Stendhal and I think I had an edge in the last one. But nobody's going to get me in any ring with Mr. Tolstoy unless I am crazy or I keep getting better."

(Add to the Indian talk, metaphors, and nicknames, the patronizing habit of calling Tolstoy Mr. Tolstoy.)

On dialogue: "When the people are talking, I can hardly write fast enough to keep up with it, but with an almost unbearable high manifold pressure. I put more inches on than she will take, and then fly her as near as I know to how she should be flown, only flying as crazy as really good pilots fly crazy sometimes. Most of the time flying conservatively but with an awfully fast airplane that makes up for the conservatism. That way you live longer, I mean your writing lives longer."

Then Hemingway says something which he repeats at odd moments during the two days Miss Ross is with him:

"How do you like it now, gentlemen?"

Miss Ross comments: "The question seemed to have some special significance for him, but he did not bother to explain it." Some years later Hemingway developed paranoid delusions. Was this an early symptom? If not, what *did* he mean? Was it more Hemingway verbal tomfoolery? We can only speculate, but Miss Ross's profile describes a disturbed man, his exuberance forced, his braggadocio labored.

A few minutes later he says it again. He is talking about the profanity in his new novel. He says he personally talked "gently." Then be brags about the new book (which, most agree, was the worst he ever wrote): "I think I've got 'Farewell' [to Arms] beat in this one. It hasn't got the youth and the ignorance."

"How do you like it now, gentlemen?"

Miss Dietrich arrives. She is greeted enthusiastically. "The Kraut's the best that ever came into the ring," Hemingway says, handing her a glass of champagne. Later Miss Dietrich says she sometimes washes her granddaughter's diapers. "Daughter, you are hitting them with the bases loaded," Hemingway says.

The next morning Miss Ross receives an urgent telephone call from Hemingway asking her to come to the hotel. He was wearing, she recalls, an "orange plaid bathrobe that looked too small for him," and had a glass of champagne in one hand. "He said he had been up since daybreak, writing. He always woke at daybreak, he explained, because his eyelids were thin and his eyes sensitive to light. He took a box of pills from his bathrobe pocket and downed them with a mouthful of champagne." (The pills were not identified; they might have been for his high blood pressure.)

It was still morning but he had finished one bottle of champagne and was starting on another. He talked more about writing: "The test of a book is how much good stuff you can throw away," he said, "When I am writing it, I am just as proud as a goddamn lion. I use the oldest words in the English language. People think I am an ignorant bastard who doesn't know the $10 words. I know the $10 words. There are older and better words and if you arrange them in the proper combination you make it stick." He pointed out that he was the only Hemingway boy who never went to college (there was only one other boy of the six Hemingway children, but perhaps Hemingway was including his father, a physician). He seemed obsessed with comparing himself with other writers:

"Mr. Flaubert, who always threw them perfectly straight, hard, high, and inside. Then Mr. Baudelaire, that I learned my knuckle ball from, and Mr. Rimbaud, who never threw a fast ball in his life. Mr. Gide and Mr. Valéry, I couldn't learn from. I think Mr. Valéry was too smart for me. . . ."

He changes the subject and talks about his cats. He has fifty-two cats. One cat eats everything that human beings eat and is unhappy because Hemingway won't give him blood pressure tablets and Seconal (this is the first hint we have that Hemingway used Seconal). "I am a strange old man," he says. "How do you like it now, gentlemen?"

Hemingway returns to writing: "It is sort of fun to be fifty and feel you are going to defend the title again. I won it in the twenties, defended it in the thirties and the forties and I don't mind at all defending it in the fifties."

Lunch is ordered up to the room. Hemingway says they cannot have lunch without wine and they wait until the waiter brings it before starting to eat. Before leaving the room to go shopping,

Hemingway finishes off the champagne. "The half bottle of champagne is the enemy of man," he says.

Shortly before that Hemingway has talked about death. "Who the hell should care about saving his soul when it is a man's duty to lose it intelligently, the way you would sell a position you were defending, if you could not hold it, as expensively as possible, trying to make it the most expensive position that was ever sold. It isn't hard to die." (Add to sports and aviation metaphors, military metaphors.) Hemingway has eleven years to live before he will fire off both barrels of a shotgun propped against his soft palate.

Out on the street Ross describes another Hemingway mannerism: "A flock of pigeons flew by. He stopped, looked up, and aimed an imaginary rifle at them. He pulled the trigger and then looked disappointed. Very difficult shot."

It is cold and he says he hates the cold. Later he says he hates the rain. This is a man who has hunted, fished, and boated in the worst weather imaginable. Perhaps he does hate the cold and the rain. Psychiatry has a term, *counterphobia*, which describes people who do precisely the things they most dislike or most fear. It requires no excess of Freudian speculation to diagnose Hemingway as a possible lifelong, world-class counterphobe.

Shopping, he ranges in mood from high to low. In an elevator a "middle-aged woman standing next to him stared at his straggly white beard with obvious alarm and disapproval." "Good Christ!" Hemingway says, suddenly in the silence of the elevator, and the middle-aged woman looks at her feet. A few minutes later he runs into a friend and says, excitedly, "All of a sudden I found I could write wonderful again." Then they talk about a man who caught a marlin.

"How do you like it now, gentlemen?" Hemingway asks no one in particular.

The next day Miss Ross and the Hemingways go to the Metropolitan Museum. Hemingway hums to himself and watches the street. In the lobby he pulls a silver flask from a pocket, unscrews its top, and takes a long drink. For the next two hours, between pictures, Hemingway takes swigs from the flask. He says he has learned a lot from painters. "I can make a landscape like Mr. Paul Cézanne." He says he has learned a lot from Mr. Johann Sebastian

Bach. He says he uses the word *and* repeatedly just as "Mr. Johann Sebastian Bach" would use a note repeatedly when writing counterpoint.

Finally, he says, "Pickles, don't you think two hours is a long time looking at pictures?" Everybody agrees and they start back to the hotel.

It is still raining when they come from the museum. Miss Ross quotes Hemingway: "Goddamn, I hate to go out in the rain. Goddamn, I hate to get wet."

This, from the country's most famous big-game hunter.

The profile ends back at the hotel where Hemingway has lunch with his publisher, Charles Scribner. Not much happens, but Hemingway says one thing which may reveal something of his mental state, and the profile ends on an amusing note.

"Shooting gives me a good feeling," Hemingway says. "A lot of it is being together and friendly instead of feeling that you are in some place where everybody hates you and wishes you ill." Early paranoia? Who can say.

Hemingway then gets a call from someone offering him $4,000 to pose as a Man of Distinction, an advertising campaign for a brand of whiskey. "I told them I wouldn't drink the stuff for $4,000," he says. "I told them I was a champagne man. Am trying to be a good guy, but it's a difficult trade. What you win in Boston, you lose in Chicago."

When her profile appeared in the *New Yorker* in the spring of 1950, Miss Ross received some angry mail. Some readers very much disliked Hemingway and assumed she felt the same way. Others felt she was ridiculing or attacking him. Others, she believed, wanted him to be somebody else—"probably themselves."

The profile was later published as a book and Miss Ross wrote at great length about how much she liked and admired Ernest Hemingway. She said such things as the following:

His compliments were straight and honest, and they were designed to make people feel good. . . . He was generous in his conversation. He didn't hoard his ideas or his thoughts or his humors or his opinions. He was so inventive that he probably had the feeling there was plenty more where that came from. But whatever his feeling might have been, he would have talked as he did out of sheer generosity. He offered so much in what he said, and always with fun and with sharp understanding and compassion and sensitivity. When he talked, he was free. The sound and the contact and the content were marvelously alive.

This is *not* the Hemingway described by everyone. Even his closest friends knew he could be mean, petty, vain, even cruel. His patriarchal-looking beard may have given him an "air of saintliness and innocence"—to use Miss Ross's phrase—but Hemingway was no saint and he was innocent only in the sense of having never been convicted of a serious crime. His good side, which he had, was perhaps described effusively by Miss Ross as an act of apology: her portrait of Hemingway is savage. The man is made to appear ridiculous—and he wasn't a ridiculous man. But he might have been drunk, very drunk. Miss Ross dutifully records every drink she personally observed, but the "invisible" drinks in the life of an alcoholic greatly exceed those consumed for the public record, and only Hemingway really knew how much he had been drinking.

What was Hemingway's reaction to the Ross profile? When he heard about the angry mail, he told Miss Ross not to worry about it. People, he said, got things all mixed up. "Some people," Miss Ross wrote, "couldn't understand his enjoying himself and his not being really spooky; they couldn't understand his being a serious writer without being pompous."

She was obviously feeling guilty and Hemingway was being tolerant. Hemingway, in her profile, was not just spooky; he was obnoxious and sometimes plain nuts. A.E. Hotchner also wrote about the New York visit. Hemingway threw a party in his hotel suite and there, "off to one side, with a stenographer's pad in her lap, sat Lillian Ross . . . taking rapid shorthand notes for a profile of Ernest. . . ."

"It was a shorter hand than any of us knew," Hemingway told Hotchner a few months later.

Hemingway lived in Cuba for many years. When Castro took

over the country Hemingway left quickly and left behind a houseful of letters, manuscripts, photographs, and other documents. These became available to the general public for the first time late in 1984. For more about the life and work and drinking of Ernest Hemingway, we now turn to this biographical windfall from Cuba.

Starting in the 1950s, travel guides of Europe almost invariably included Ernest Hemingway in the index. Turning to the page listed, one found that in Venice, Hemingway drank at Harry's Bar; in Paris, at the Ritz Bar; in Madrid, at Chicote's Bar. It is never explained why tourists should be interested in Hemingway's favorite bars (no other literary figure receives this attention), but writers of travel books know their audience and indeed tourists by the thousands and maybe millions have sought out the bars where Hemingway drank and maybe even had one themselves to commemorate the occasion. Perhaps one would be closer to explaining the American writers' fatal attraction to alcohol in the twentieth century, and the corresponding attraction of readers to alcoholic writers, if one understood why so many tourists would pass up Notre Dame to peek into the window of the Ritz Bar.

In any case, Hemingway's watering holes have been never more celebrated elsewhere than in Cuba, where he lived for twenty-two years on a farm outside Havana. American tourists are just starting to go back to Cuba and great numbers flock to a bar called the Floridita in Havana. The Floridita had been around a century or so by the time Hemingway discovered it but Hemingway made the place famous. The Floridita had obtained a reputation for having invented the *double* frozen daiquiri (sometimes called the Hemingway Daiquiri, or Papa Doble). Requested by most tourists, a Papa Doble was compounded of two and one-half jiggers of Bacardi White Label Rum, the juice of two limes and half a grapefruit, and six drops of maraschino, all placed in an electric mixer over shaved ice, whirled vigorously, and served foaming in large goblets.

Hemingway once drank sixteen in one night (the "house record"). If the story is true—and there were witnesses—he consumed some 60 ounces of 80-proof rum, the juice of 32 limes and 8 grapefruits, and 96 drops of maraschino. And if the witnesses are to be believed, he walked away on his own power.

Hemingway didn't *always* drink sixteen daiquiris. Often the figure was about half that. We know this from a visit paid Hemingway in 1948 by A.E. Hotchner, then an editor for *Cosmopolitan* magazine. Hotchner had come to Cuba to talk Hemingway into writing a piece called "The Future of Literature." They met at the Floridita Bar. They were immediately served up with Papa Dobles. Hotchner had seven and was wobbly. Hemingway had at least that number and took a drink with him for the road, sitting in the front seat of the stationwagon next to the chauffeur. They met early the next morning to go fishing. The boat was well supplied with alcoholic beverages. Hemingway put some tequila on ice and they later took a sip to see if it was cold enough. There is no mention of how much tequila they drank. The fishing went well.

Hotchner's visit took place nearly two years before Hemingway's visit to New York where he was interviewed by Lillian Ross. He must have aged considerably between forty-eight and fifty. Hotchner says that he looked in great shape.

His hair was dark with gray highlights, flecked white at the temples, and he had a heavy moustache that ran past the corners of his mouth, but no beard. He was massive. Not in height, for he was only an inch over six feet, nor in weight, but in impact [in other accounts he is said to be five feet eleven inches, but maybe he shrank; people do]. Most of his 200 pounds were concentrated above his waist: he had square, heavy shoulders, large hugely muscled arms . . . a deep chest, a belly-rise but no hips or thighs. Something played off him—he was intense, electrokinetic, but in control, a racehorse reined in.

Hotchner and Hemingway were close friends for the rest of Hemingway's life. Hotchner's book, *Papa Hemingway,* may not be accurate in every factual detail but traces the clinical course of Hemingway from the healthy heroic-drinking days of his late forties to his decline in his fifties and death by suicide at sixty-one.

When word reached Havana that Ernest Hemingway had committed suicide, a young journalist named Norberto Fuentes was assigned to write a story about the Hemingway whom Cubans had known for more than two decades. Fuentes did a bangup job. Over a seven-year period he must have interviewed everyone in Cuba who had ever met, seen, or heard of Hemingway. This included Hemingway's personal physicians, the crews of his fishing boats, his cronies from the cockfights, the cooks and the help in the bars, his rum-drinking companions on nights of revelry. In his hurry to leave Cuba, Hemingway had left behind practically everything. His large handsome house, high on a windswept hill overlooking Havana and the Gulf Stream, surrounded by rural poverty, looks as if Ernest and Mary might walk in at any moment. Unopened letters lie on the bed. The cellar is stocked with wine casks and whiskey cases. On the "drink table" Hemingway built next to his chair the bottles still wait for Papa's morning, afternoon, and evening drinks. Most of the nine thousand books remain. Only the valuable paintings have been taken. When Mary Hemingway donated the house to Cuba, she was permitted to take the paintings, which today are probably worth millions.

Only the bathroom differed from earlier descriptions of it. Hemingway's bathroom, Hotchner wrote, was "large and cluttered with medicines and medical paraphernalia which bulged out of the cabinet and onto all surfaces; the room was badly in need of paint but painting was impossible because the walls were covered with inked records, written in Ernest's careful hand, of dated blood-pressure counts, and weights, prescription numbers, and other medical and pharmaceutical intelligence." (Like many writers, Hemingway was a hypochondriac.)

Fuentes had access to letters, articles, and scraps of manuscripts never before available to Hemingway scholars. When he finally published a book on his findings, *Hemingway in Cuba*, in 1984, it included more than a hundred pages of unpublished letters and scores of photographs. For many of us who thought we knew everything about Hemingway there was to know, it came as a most pleasant surprise. The book ends with an inventory of the Hemingway home. On the floor of Hemingway's bedroom are a lion skin and head. On the wall: a buffalo head, a map of Cuba, and a jar that holds a frog preserved in Formalin. Elsewhere: his slippers, a whistle to attract ducks, a liquor license from Idaho, a shoehorn, and a framed picture of Lillian Ross, the lady who slaughtered Hemingway in the *New Yorker*. Hemingway had a more forgiving nature than was generally supposed.

The book is interesting and valuable, but for the true Hemingway buff the inventory will leave the strongest sense of life's futility and sadness; in short, a Hemingway feeling.

Hemingway has been virtually canonized in Cuba: his house a museum, his former hotel room closed to the public, a strip of coastal water called the Hemingway Mile, a bust of Hemingway over his barstool in the Floridita. It seems all the Cubans have a Hemingway story. They are often contradictory.

The stories most contradictory are the ones about his drinking. Everyone agrees that he drank often and heavy but most seem to feel he could hold it. According to his personal physician and friend, Herrera Sotolongo, quoted in a recent biography, Hemingway "drank a lot, but for those of us accustomed to the life of a heavy drinker in countries where drinking is taken very seriously, he didn't drink *that much*." When he did drink too much, the doctor said, he was totally incapable of writing.

Hemingway drank heaviest, Sotolongo recalls, when he fell in love with a young Italian countess and started to quarrel with his fourth wife, Mary. Sotolongo told Hemingway, "If you keep on drinking this way you won't even be able to write your name." During this period, according to the doctor, Hemingway was always drunk. "It was his bad time, when we had our falling out. One day I told him, 'Look, kid, you have turned into a drunkard and I hate that. If you don't change, we'll have to stop being friends.'" Sotolongo even removed the guns from Hemingway's house because the Hemingways were threatening to shoot each other.

In the 1930s Hemingway wrote a Russian friend that alcohol gave him the only relief available from the "mechanical oppression" of modern life. In his unfinished novel, *Islands in the Stream*, the hero also fights "mechanical oppression" from the back seat of his car where he drinks while looking at the squalor of the Havana of the forties.

What kind of drinker was Hemingway on a daily basis? The pattern changed, of course, but during the years Hemingway was actually in Cuba—not covering the civil war in Spain or liberating Paris or arguing with his editors in New York—the Cuban consensus is that Hemingway was a fairly consistent drinker except when he was inconsistent. Fuentes describes the following pattern:

To begin the day, Hemingway would drink two highballs or Tom Collinses in the swimming pool, or have whiskey and soda, or plain whiskey on the rocks. Later he would have wine with his lunch.

He napped until 4:00 or 5:00, and then read while waiting for dinner; he usually did not drink again until he sat down at the table. He liked to read again between dinner and bedtime, and this was accompanied by a little wine.

On an average day at the Vigía [farm], three or four friends could help Ernest consume three or four bottles of whiskey. It never seemed to be too much for him.

Sometimes he varied his drinks. He liked to change. Whiskey, gin, campari, Tom Collins, tequila. He also drank different wines: Tavel, his favorite French rosé, then Chianti in the straw bottle, four or five litres with dinner. He liked to serve the wine himself. He held the bottle by the neck while he poured. This was awkward but he justified it by saying: The bottles, by the neck. Women by the waist.

When did Hemingway find time to write? Hemingway's version is somewhat different from the above. According to Hemingway (in letters and elsewhere), he awoke every morning at sunrise (those thin eyelids), had a cup of coffee, and then went to work standing up, barefoot, in his shorts at a waist-high bookcase transformed into a desk. He alternately typed on his Royal typewriter and wrote in longhand. His goal was five hundred words a day. It took him most of the morning. The afternoon was spent relaxing. This usually meant going to a bar and drinking with friends. Other times he took his boat out on the gulf and fished for marlin. He had a well-stocked bar on the boat and presumably did some drinking there too. In any case, except for wine with dinner, his drinking was mostly finished for the day. True he would sip some more wine into the evening while reading, but was in bed by eleven. He awoke refreshed and ready to write.

Hemingway suggests this was a routine carried out religiously. According to cooks and other household help, it was not always so religious. He often didn't get up until midmorning or noon, even on days when he was on a writing project. Hangover is the most likely explanation.

What was Hemingway's attitude toward his drinking? He expressed it often, but not always the same way. According to Fuentes, more than once his drinking companions heard Hemingway's advice: "Drink all you want, but don't be a drunken shit. I drink and get drunk every day, but I never bother anyone." (Apparently he forgot the fistfights in the Floridita, Toots Shor's in New York, and elsewhere.)

In World War II, while roughing it on the European front, he wrote his wife that

> we haven't had any liquor for two days and you'll be happy to know that I am all the same without it as with it—think maybe steadier and better—although I have loved it, needed it, and many times it has saved one's damned reason, self-respect, and whatall . . . besides great pleasure and I love it. We always called it the Giant Killer and nobody who has not had to deal with the Giant many, many times has any right to speak against the Giant Killer.

In his midfifties, Hemingway became jaundiced. His Cuban physician friend diagnosed the problem as hepatitis. He said the cause was probably not alcohol but recommended that Hemingway drink less. Hemingway referred to this period as that of the "new dry law." His jaundice was *one* problem he couldn't solve with alcohol. According to Fuentes, a liter of any alcoholic beverage usually "helped him to face storms, wars and moments of loneliness." But not hepatitis. He had to stay dry and in bed.

Hemingway's doctor did not believe alcohol had caused the hepatitis and Hemingway went to considerable lengths to prove the innocence of alcohol, reading textbooks in search of scientific evidence showing that alcohol lacked a direct toxic effect on the liver. (It probably does.) In any case, Hemingway's attack of hepatitis took many years to be cured, and he may still have had liver damage at the time of his death. A year or so before his death he was observed to be jaundiced, but this was preceded by two airplane crashes in which he had received serious injuries. There is nothing in the public record indicating that Hemingway was diagnosed as having cirrhosis, although hospitals like the Mayo Clinic, where Hemingway was a patient, maintain strict confidentiality about these matters. Nor is there record that he was ever hospitalized for treatment of alcoholism, or had grand-mal seizures from drinking. Hemingway, to the end, excluded himself from the long list of American writers who were alcoholic.

Should *we* exclude Hemingway from the list of American writers who were alcoholic? Ultimately this depends on the definition of alcoholism. Of the Americans who have won the Nobel Prize in literature, John Steinbeck is the one most often described as a heavy drinker but not alcoholic. Hemingway is on some lists of alcoholics and not on others. In the chapter on Steinbeck, I discuss the definition of alcoholism at some length and present current diagnostic criteria to help the reader decide whether Steinbeck was technically alcoholic. Did Hemingway fit the standard medical definition of alcoholism? The answer is that he did.

Like Faulkner and Lowry, Hemingway could control his drinking over long stretches. He was more successful in doing this when he was deeply immersed in a writing project. Lillian Ross, feeling guilty about her profile, said that Hemingway was "heroically and uncorruptedly and uncompromisingly occupied day after day with writing as hard as *he could* and as well as *he could* until the day he died." This is simply not true. Hemingway had long arid periods when he produced little or nothing. Nevertheless, his dedication to writing was total and consuming; it could keep him sober for long periods, although never completely dry. In the last few years of his life, when his health was poor and doctors told him to stop altogether, he reduced his drinking to combinations of one cocktail and two wines, or two wines and two Scotches, or one Scotch and one daiquiri, but never stopped completely. No doubt, people who saw him during the times of control concluded he was not alcoholic.

Nevertheless, alcohol dominated his life. He once told his friend Hotchner, "I have been drunk 1,547 times in my life, but never in the morning," yet, in a book called *The Hemingway Women* by Bernice Kert, his wives referred constantly to the vodka and tequila with which he would start the day, the Bloody Marys at noon, and the daiquiris and Scotch and oceans of wine that filled the afternoons and early evenings. He was almost always in bed early and up at six on the days when he didn't drink, and from six to twelve he usually wrote. He was often irascible and even cruel, and one never knew whether it was the booze or the hangover causing it.

True, he never checked into a hospital to dry out, but his two hospitalizations at Mayo Clinic in the last year of his life were for depression and for a condition possibly related to his drinking: paranoia. He believed that his phone was bugged and the FBI after him, and that he was poor when indeed he was rich. He had hallucinations. He had two courses of electroconvulsive therapy at Mayo Clinic, but the delusions never went away, nor did the depression. Three months passed between his two admissions and he killed himself a few days after leaving the hospital the second time.

Speculation about his diagnosis no doubt remains in a locked file in Rochester. One possibility, however, was chronic alcoholic hallucinosis. This is a rare disorder that occurs in alcoholics who stop drinking and then develop a chronic condition resembling paranoid schizophrenia. The main symptoms are hallucinations and delusions of persecution. These symptoms also occur sometimes when people become severely depressed, and there is no question that Hemingway was depressed in the last years of his life. Still, the delusions seemed more persistent than the depression and did not vanish after shock therapy (which one would expect if the primary disorder had been depression).

Hemingway's paranoia seems to have begun at about the time he started reducing his alcohol intake for health reasons. (The nature of the health problems is not entirely clear, but high blood pressure was one problem and persistent hepatitis may have been another.) At any rate, the appearance of paranoid symptoms at a time when an alcoholic reduces his drinking leads to an interesting theory espoused by Malcolm Lowry. Lowry believed that alcohol *prevented* him from having a nervous breakdown. "I drink *through* a breakdown," he wrote, "not *into* one." In his letter to Mary from the war front in Europe, mentioned earlier, Hemingway maintained that liquor had saved his "reason, self-respect, and whatall." He said that liquor was a Giant Killer and "nobody who has not had to deal with the Giant many, many times has any right to speak against the

Giant Killer." Hemingway's Giant Killer theory will be discussed in chapter nine, but it had *personal* meanings beyond its applicability to writers generally.

What was Hemingway's Giant that alcohol killed? On one occasion Hemingway had identified the Giant as "the drive for success": it was the hunger for prestige, fame, and money that drove all those writers to drink. Like everyone who is ill, Hemingway was always trying to explain the cause of his illness. His success theory may be true, somewhat true, or not true at all. Hemingway's Giant may have been depression. It may have been loneliness. (He once told Lillian Ross that he wrote many letters so he would receive letters back and letters made him feel less lonely.)

The Giant may have been fear. In the Ross profile, his justification for constant activity was to avoid ending up in one room, never moving. Much of Hemingway's derring-do suggests, to the psychiatrist, counterphobia—which is overcoming fear by exaggerated acts of courage.

Or perhaps the Giant was the "mechanical oppression" of modern life which, Hemingway said, could be relieved only by alcohol. Like Lowry, what peace he could find seemed attainable only in primitive surroundings, although there are vast differences between Hemingway's handsome house on the hill and Lowry's beach shack, and whereas British Columbia seemed to reduce Lowry's drinking, Cuba seemed to increase Hemingway's (if anything).

Finally, perhaps the Giant was Hemingway's awareness of a cruel streak in his nature that coexisted with a sweetness and gentleness and generosity which were the Hemingway most people knew. The cruel streak was real and sometimes out of control. *Hemingway in Cuba* gives some chilling examples. Here is one:

Hemingway believed that plants and trees should grow without restraint. His wife Mary once permitted a gardener to cut off the root of a tree growing under the house. Hemingway was enraged. Every morning, for many days, Mary had to do penance. With Hemingway watching she had to kneel in front of the tree and ask forgiveness. (The story may be apocryphal but it *sounds* true in the context of other events.)

Hemingway's cruelty toward other writers, particularly Fitzgerald, is well known. But it also shows up in papers found in his Cuban farmhouse. Faulkner, for example, was once mildly critical of Hemingway, saying that Hemingway always "stayed within the limits of what he knew . . . and never tried to reach the impossible." Hemingway's macho was under attack—no other writer, in his opinion, took greater risks in life and art than he—and he responded with one of the cruelest letters ever written by one great writer about another:

> . . . [tell him] on his death-bed if possible, that I think he is a chicken-shit man who had great talent as a writer and for lack of application, rummy-hood, Hollywood and the usual faults of the professional southerner turned out to be a morning glory. But never did he fault to turn up in N.Y. for the launching of a new book, nor to kiss the ass of those who gave him prizes. Tell him I touted him all over Europe for years as the greatest writer in the U.S. because I was sorry for him in his rummy-hood and hoped he could get where he could make a living without whoring in Hollywood. Tell him he is a whore and a sad cunt with a mellifluous voice and all the unexpended corn-directed talent of the Southern coward.

Hemingway's delight in cockfights, bullfights, prizefights—in shooting pigeons, Germans, wildlife of every description—must be viewed side by side with his generosity to his friends, to the poor, and to his family (*except* his mother), and also with his sentimental affection for cats, dogs, and trees growing under his house. The Giant, in short, may have been his awareness of something barbaric in his makeup, something unacceptable to the man he thought he was and wished himself to be. Most of the time there was a precarious armistice between the two sides, and alcohol helped keep the peace.

His best writing was about death and violence. None other could write battle scenes better than Hemingway. As such, "The Retreat from Caporetto" and "The Fight on the Hilltop," chapters from two of his best novels, are incomparable. His ambivalence about war clearly reflects the opposing sides of his personality. In his introduction to *Men at War* he says, "I have seen much war in my lifetime and I hate it profoundly. But there are worse things than war; and all of them come with defeat. The more you hate war, the more you know that once you are forced into it, for whatever reason it may be, you have to win it and get rid of the people that made it. . . ."

Then, in a wonderful paragraph, Hemingway describes the difference between a warrior and a writer.

A good soldier does not worry. He knows that nothing happens until it actually happens and you live your life up until then. Danger only exists at the moment of danger. To live properly in war, the individual eliminates all such things as potential danger. Then a thing is only bad when it is bad. It is neither bad before nor after. Cowardice, as distinguished from panic, is almost always simply a lack of ability to suspend the functioning of the imagination. Learning to suspend your imagination and live completely in the very second of the present minute, with no before and no after, is the greatest gift a soldier can acquire. It, naturally, is the opposite of all those gifts a writer should have. This is what makes good writing by good soldiers such a rare thing and why it is so prized when we have it.

In Hemingway we had it and it was much prized, as it should have been. But the strain on the writer can only be surmised.

Or the Giant may have been something else, something not even suspected here. Hemingway may not have had the foggiest idea what it was, but he is utterly convincing about its existence.

Hemingway was sometimes called a manic-depressive, and there is reason to believe that that was his diagnosis at the Mayo Clinic. One problem with heavy drinkers is that they become depressed and one never knows whether drinking causes the depression or depression causes the drinking. Psychiatrists agree that a heavy drinker must stop drinking before a diagnosis can be made.

Hemingway did, in the last few years of his life, reduce the amount he drank to the point where an alcohol-induced depression seems unlikely. He still became depressed. His health was poor, his writing powers were failing, but this happens to many people who find other solutions than suicide.

His father, not an alcoholic, committed suicide when he was depressed, and depression runs in families. Ernest may have carried the genes (nobody really knows, of course, whether genes are responsible).

Hemingway had mood swings, some long and severe enough to

be clinical depressions. No clear-cut manic episodes are reported, but he could easily have been called hypomanic (mildly manic) much of his life, although "zest for living" is perhaps a better term. Beneath the zest for living, however, was a pervasive sadness that would break through, and, again, one wonders whether the drinking was behind it or an inherited tendency to depression.

The Czechs have a word, *litost*, which designates a feeling of grief, remorse, and indefinable longing. According to the celebrated Czech writer Milan Kundera, "The first syllable, which is long and stressed, sounds like the wail of an abandoned dog . . . a state of torment caused by a sudden insight into one's own miserable self." Nothing brings on *litost* so much as a hangover, and Hemingway must have been drunk or hung over much of his adult life.

In a beautiful chapter in *A Moveable Feast*, Hemingway tells about spending an idyllic day with his first wife, Hadley, in their twenties in Paris, when they had gone to the races, had a picnic with wine, and then decided to splurge at a good restaurant. "It was a wonderful meal," he writes, "but when we had finished and there was no question of hunger any more, the feeling that had been like hunger . . . was still there when we caught the bus home. It was there when we came in the room and after we had gone to bed and made love in the dark, it was there. When I woke with the windows open and the moonlight on the roofs of the tall houses, it was there." This was Hemingway's *litost*. He had it all his life. Money, love, fame, adventure, alcohol—nothing dispelled it for long.

People couldn't understand why he committed suicide. "On July 2, 1961," wrote Hotchner,

a writer whom many critics called the greatest writer of this century, a man who had a zest for life and adventure as big as his genius, a winner of the Nobel Prize and the Pulitzer Prize, a soldier of fortune with a home in Idaho's Sawtooth Mountains, where he hunted in the winter, an apartment in New York, a specially rigged yacht to fish the Gulf Stream, an available apartment at the Ritz in Paris and the Gritti in Venice, a solid marriage, no serious physical illness, good friends everywhere—on that July day, that man, the envy of other men, put a shotgun to his head and killed himself.

This must have been written before Hotchner knew about the *litost* lurking behind the zest for life.

The alcoholic, Alan Bold wrote, can use his artistic ability to confront *litost* with creativity. "If, however, he succumbs to *litost*, he admits defeat and takes to ruinous drinking."

At sixty-one Hemingway had foresworn ruinous drinking. He had only one other option and took it.

Bibliographical Note

Lillian Ross's profile on Hemingway was later republished as a book, *Portrait of Hemingway* (New York: Simon & Schuster, 1961).

Hemingway in Cuba by Norberto Fuentes, reviewing much new information about the writer, was published by Lyle Stuart, Inc. (Secaucus, N.J.), in 1984. Gabriel García Márquez provided a splendid introduction.

A.E. Hotchner's *Papa Hemingway* (New York: Random House, 1966) is as readable as a novel and provides firsthand information about Hemingway's fifties in Havana, New York, Paris, Venice, Madrid, Rochester (Minn.), and, finally, Ketchum (Idaho). Hemingway's opinion of Castro receives somewhat different versions in the books by Fuentes and Hotchner.

Recommended is Bernice Kert's *The Hemingway Women* (New York: Norton, 1986). The book is long, detailed, beautifully written, and best read together with a collection of Hemingway's stories and novels, as, one by one, his women appear in them. The women are, by and large, a remarkable lot. In later life Hemingway called his mother a bitch and blamed her for his father's suicide, but there is nothing in this book to justify such talk. Instead, she emerges as an indomitable spirit who loved her six children and became something of a musician and artist in days when women usually didn't become these things. Three of his wives were from St. Louis. The first, Hadley, was nine years older and had the curious mother-daughter, lover-victim relationship with Ernest that he had with all his women, except for Martha Gelhorn, who finally could take only so much and left him. Three of his wives were professional writers, but only Gelhorn kept writing; the others abandoned themselves entirely to Ernest and his work. He was tender and brutal alternately. Even after divorces, the wives felt kindly toward him.

There are more books in the library about Hemingway than about any other writer except Poe and Shakespeare. Among those used in preparation for this chapter was Carlos Baker's definitive biography of Hemingway, *Ernest Hemingway: A Life Story* (New York: Charles Scribner's Sons, 1969).

Two books by the family, Leicester Hemingway's *My Brother Ernest Hemingway* (Cleveland: World Publishing, 1962) and Mary Hemingway's *How It Was* (New York: Knopf, 1976), limn in the background. Anthony Burgess's *Ernest Hemingway and His World* (New York: Charles Scribner's Sons, 1978) takes a writer's eye view of the subject. Hemingway's introduction to his anthology, *Men at War,* was published by Crown (New York) in 1942.

Three full-scale, ambitious new biographies of Hemingway appeared in the mid-1980s: *Hemingway: A Biography* by Jeffrey Meyers (New York: Harper & Row, 1985); *The Young Hemingway* by Michael Reynolds (New York: Oxford University Press, 1986); and *Hemingway* by Kenneth Lynn (New York: Simon & Schuster, 1987). None added much new information about Hemingway's drinking, except to confirm that his addiction to alcohol was serious. Lynn contributes some new medical information. In his late forties Hemingway was diagnosed as having hypertension (his blood pressure was 215/125) and was told to lose weight (he tipped the scales at 256). A combination of pills and weight loss lowered the blood pressure but not for long, and throughout his fifties he had increasingly serious health problems, including, by one count, liver and kidney disease, diabetes mellitus, and hemochromatosis (a rare disease characterized by widespread deposits of an iron-containing substance through the body, leading to cirrhosis, bronzed skin, and diabetes). We even learn his cholesterol count (380) and the fact that his liver was visible to a casual observer ("You could see the bulge of it stand out from his body like a long, fat leech," recalled George Plimpton from his meetings with Hemingway in the fifties). As his health got worse so did his mood. A companion on an African safari wrote that "he was drunk the whole time," although he rarely showed it. "Just became merrier, more lovable, more bullshitty. Without drink he was morose, silent and depressed."

The Lynn biography also provides another candidate for the role of *Giant*, which Hemingway was trying to kill by drinking. As a child, Hemingway and his slightly older sister were often mistaken for twins and, indeed, his mother encouraged the error. She had Ernie and the sister cut their hair in the same butch style and was sexually provocative to her cute little blond-haired boy. All this, in Lynn's view, contributed to a confusion of sexual identity, with Ernest never quite clear which sex he was supposed to be. All of this was unconscious, of course, and Hemingway was as militantly virile as he was intolerant of homosexuality. This confusion finally emerged in his posthumously published novel, *The Garden of Eden*, wherein the protagonist and his lover play sexual games that involve changing gender. All of this makes good Freudian sense and Lynn is right when he says that no reader of *The Garden of Eden* will probably view Hemingway quite the same thereafter. Was his confused sexual identity related to his depression and ferocious drinking? As always, one can only speculate.

4

STEINBECK
The Dog That Didn't Bark

*The alcoholic is a person who can take it
or leave it, so he takes it.*

Charles Jackson

The first three American men who won the Nobel Prize in literature were Sinclair Lewis, Eugene O'Neill, and William Faulkner: all alcoholic. The fourth was Hemingway, who disliked being called alcoholic but probably was one. The fifth was John Steinbeck, a "heavy drinker."

When people talk about Steinbeck's drinking they usually make a point of saying that he was a heavy drinker but not alcoholic. What is the basis for the distinction? Presumably all alcoholics are heavy drinkers, but not all heavy drinkers are alcoholic. What must a heavy drinker *do* besides drink heavily to qualify as an alcoholic?

It boils down to definition. The condition called alcoholism needs a definition. Simply calling alcoholism a disease doesn't help. The dictionary defines *disease* as the absence of health; it defines *health* as freedom from disease. Actually, diseases are problems that inspire people to see doctors; no other definition fits historically.

Alcoholism, today, is defined by problems. If you drink and have problems, you are alcoholic. If you drink and have no problems, you are not alcoholic.

Disagreement arises in deciding how *many* problems. Many normal drinkers have had problems from drinking—hangovers, memory lapses, quarrels—but the problems are not frequent or serious. How frequent or serious must problems be before a person qualifies as an alcoholic?

Here is the way alcoholism researchers do it: they draw up a list of alcohol-related problems and if a person has X number of problems the person is called alcoholic. The number is arbitrary, a convention agreed upon by the researchers. Nevertheless, the definition is specific and when the term *alcoholism* is used, people more or less agree upon its meaning.

Did Steinbeck have problems from drinking? If so, how frequent? How serious? Did he have sufficient problems to fulfill today's research criteria for alcoholism?

Except for people who knew him well, this was impossible to answer until recently. Steinbeck was a private man; he wrote little about himself and never about his drinking. The two or three thin biographies that existed until recently were mostly about his books.

In 1984, however, an 1,116-page tome called *The True Adventures of John Steinbeck, Writer* appeared in bookstores and, suddenly, more was known about John Steinbeck than was ever known before. John Kenneth Galbraith wrote: "There will not be another book like it nor will we need one." Carlos Baker wrote: "[The author] has . . . projected a far fuller and more detailed picture of John Steinbeck's personality and actions and interests than anyone else has done or probably will ever do."

Both jacket blurbs give off a whiff of readers' fatigue as well as imply—unintentionally, no doubt—that Steinbeck didn't deserve so much attention (and surely will never receive it again). In any case, Jackson J. Benson, the author, spent thirteen years writing the book. He interviewed hundreds of people, pored over papers and letters in a half dozen university libraries, and had the cooperation of Steinbeck's friends and family, including all three of his wives (the second now deceased).

Because of Benson's efforts, it is now feasible to ask: Did Steinbeck have problems from drinking? How frequent? How serious?

Before taking up these questions, it is necessary to know something about John Steinbeck's life and works. Many question whether he was a great writer or even a very good writer, but he was certainly an interesting man.

Steinbeck was born in Salinas, California, in 1902 and died of heart disease in 1968. He was German on his father's side, Irish on his mother's. His father managed a flour mill and later became treasurer of Monterey County, retiring from office a year before his death in 1936. His real love was farming. He always had a garden. He was taciturn and aloof but helped John financially while he struggled to become a writer.

John's mother was a schoolteacher before her marriage. She was a warm, outgoing woman whose interest in books and music introduced John to reading and culture. She had a stroke in midlife and was paralyzed for several years before her death in 1934.

The Steinbecks had four children, three girls and John (John was the third). He attended grade school and high school in Salinas. Although a large adolescent and a massive man, he was never athletic. He was shy and didn't date. He loved animals and nature. He decided to be a writer as a freshman in high school and pursued his ambition relentlessly until his final illness.

At eighteen Steinbeck enrolled as a freshman at Stanford University and attended classes intermittently for six years, never fulfilling the requirements for graduation. His classes were mainly in classical literature, zoology, and English. He read widely and wrote constantly. He started collecting rejection slips, publishing only two stories in his college years, both in the Stanford literary magazine. He held various jobs as a ranchhand and a laborer in road gangs and sugar mills, putting himself through college with a little help from his father.

After six years at Stanford, Steinbeck went to New York and worked for a short time as a newspaper reporter but continued to support himself mainly through manual labor. Among other jobs, he pushed wheelbarrows of concrete for the construction of Madison Square Garden. He returned to the West Coast where he lived in a variety of places—Salinas, Monterey, San Francisco, Tahoe City—alternating temporary employment with periods devoted to writing. He worked as a carpenter, a department store salesman, a bench "chemist" in sugar-beet fields; spent some time in a hobo camp; and was caretaker for an estate to earn his room and board while he wrote.

Then, at twenty-seven, his first novel, *Cup of Gold*, was published and Steinbeck devoted all of his time to writing. He went to San Francisco and there met and married his first wife, Carol, who worked in the advertising department of the *San Francisco Chronicle*.

Since neither his first book nor his second made any money, he and Carol lived in a beach house in Pacific Grove, California, supported by his father, with some help from Carol.

Steinbeck finally achieved success at age thirty-three when he published *Tortilla Flat*, a bestseller about migrants and poor farmers. From then until his death at the age of sixty-six, he supported himself and his family entirely from his writing, becoming increasingly prosperous (although in later life alimony took a big bite out of his income).

After *Tortilla Flat*, Steinbeck wrote three novels widely considered to be his best: *In Dubious Battle* (1936), *Of Mice and Men* (1937), and *The Grapes of Wrath* (1939). Not only were the books well received critically but they made money as well.

Steinbeck's career went into a steady decline after 1939, although he remained productive. By the time of his death, he had written eighteen books of fiction, six nonfiction books, and seven plays and film scripts. His last real book, *Travels with Charley in Search of America*, was published in 1962, six years before his death. In 1966 he published some short essays with photographs in a book called *America and Americans*, but otherwise his writing was restricted to occasional magazine articles (and, once, some speech writing for Lyndon Johnson).

In the last two years of his life Steinbeck was so disabled from heart disease that writing was almost impossible. He had at least one stroke and repeated episodes of congestive heart failure. He also had a spinal fusion for a ruptured disc. Before his early sixties, his physical health appears to have been fairly good.

Steinbeck's personal life was divided into two parts. The first was mostly spent in California. Here, in his late twenties, he met Edward Ricketts, who had a powerful influence on his life and writings. Ricketts was a marine biologist whose studies of animal life greatly attracted Steinbeck. They made voyages together along the California coast and Steinbeck wrote about their experiences. Ricketts was the hero in three of Steinbeck's novels. When Ricketts died in 1948, Steinbeck's grief was intense and some biographers believe he lost whatever creative talent he had left because of the loss.

However, the first real change in Steinbeck's career apparently occurred in 1943 when he permanently moved from California to

New York City. He had been a war correspondent in Italy and North Africa, and then, with his second wife, Gwendolyn, became an apartment dweller in New York City. Now famous and affluent, he lived the life of a celebrity.

The marriage lasted five years and produced two sons. He met this third wife, Elaine, while she was the wife of Zachary Scott, the movie star. She took good care of him during his illnesses and it was a successful marriage.

Steinbeck traveled widely. He made one trip to Russia and wrote a book about it. He also visited Vietnam during the war; his views on the war were hawkish. As a "proletariat writer" of the thirties, he thus surprised and disillusioned many of his fans, but Steinbeck always held strong social and political views and they were not always consistent.

In 1962 Steinbeck won the Nobel Prize in literature. Many critics felt he should not have received it. Of the American literary laureates, none other was more unpopular with the critics than John Steinbeck—or more often recommended by high school teachers for their students.

Edmund Wilson and Alfred Kazin were particularly harsh in their criticism, but after the thirties almost every well-known critic found fault with Steinbeck's books. The main complaint was that he couldn't create believable characters and was oversentimental. However, Wilson and others found further reason to complain: Steinbeck's characters, they said, resembled animals more than people. Wilson came down hardest:

> Mr. Steinbeck almost always in his fiction is dealing either with the lower animals or with human beings so rudimentary that they are almost on the animal level. . . . Mr. Steinbeck does not have the effect, as Lawrence or Kipling does, of romantically raising the animals to the stature of human beings, but rather of assimilating the human beings to animals. . . . This animalizing of Mr. Steinbeck is, I believe, at the bottom of his relative unsuccess at representing human beings.

Wilson even disliked *The Grapes of Wrath:* "It is as if human sentiments and speeches had been assigned to a flock of lemmings on their way to throw themselves into the sea."

Even his admirers agreed that Steinbeck was not the writer in his forties that he had been earlier. His first biographer, Peter Lisca, blamed the decline on changes in the author's personal and public life. Steinbeck's move from California "to the fashionable East Side of New York City, with its concomitant change of personal contacts—from plain people, bums, and *paisanos*—to Broadway, Hollywood, and international celebrities—must figure in the total picture." Steinbeck became more and more a journalist and less and less a creative fiction writer, and even much of his journalism was second-rate.

After his death Steinbeck's stock with the critics continued to fall. Reviewers of the Benson biography seemed to agree with what Galbraith and Baker were implicitly suggesting: the book was awfully long and Steinbeck didn't deserve it.

Apparently, however, not many people read critics and book reviewers. No other writer in the midtwentieth century has been on the required reading list of high school and college students more than John Steinbeck. His books have been made into movies and the movies are now seen regularly on television. One book, *Of Mice and Men*, was first a novel, then a play, then a film, and finally an opera and a video cassette.

Many high school and college teachers remain Steinbeck enthusiasts. In 1968, the year of his death, Steinbeck became the subject of a journal, *The Steinbeck Quarterly,* and later was the subject of a monograph series. At least four universities have Steinbeck collections. There is a study guide for teachers who would rather read a synopsis of his books than the books, but the books *are* read, particularly, in high school, *The Red Pony* and *The Pearl*.

Why is Steinbeck so popular in the classroom, so disliked by critics? The classroom popularity in part may trace to influence of school boards: Steinbeck is considered "safe," meaning there isn't much sex or dirty language and the themes are uplifting. (It wasn't always that way. Steinbeck's neighbors in Salinas originally were as offended by the language and themes of his books as Faulkner's neighbors in Oxford were of his. After he became a celebrity and Cannery Row became a tourist attraction, it all changed; now his books are in the school library.)

The themes, indeed, may explain some of the attraction for young people, but not necessarily because they are uplifting. Actually, he had two themes, one based on biology and the other on myth. He viewed all life as a "group organism": hurrying, fighting, feeding, breeding animals related to each other. The idea permeates his novels. Joseph Fontenrose, a classical scholar who wrote a very nice little book on Steinbeck, finds a certain optimism in Steinbeck that comes from his biological reasoning: "As we rise from the tide pool through Tortilla Flat, Cannery Row, and the migrant camps, though we still see the combative and predatory characteristics of the tide pool, we see more and more cooperation, fraternity, and intelligence. The creatures of the tide pool begin to have aspirations and to reach a vision of the whole." Many critics, of course, find this sentimental nonsense, but the unsophisticated reader may sense the message and approve of it.

Steinbeck also built his stories around myth and legend. Fontenrose mentioned some of them: the Arthur cycle and biblical tales, especially the Holy Grail and Fisher King, the Garden of Eden, Cain and Abel, the Joseph story, Exodus, the Passion and Resurrection, the revolt of the angels; plus myths of dying gods, Faust, Troy and Helen, and virgin whores; and legends of city-founding. These myths and legends, after all, have been around a long time. By hitching his fictional wagon to them, Steinbeck may have assured himself of young audiences who like his books even if the critics don't.

In the early 1980s about ninety-five hundred randomly selected American adults were asked twenty questions about their use of alcohol. The study was sponsored by the National Institute of Mental Health (NIMH). Most of the questions concerned problems from drinking. From the answers, conclusions were drawn about whether the respondents were "alcoholic." (The explanation for the quotation marks comes later.)

How would John Steinbeck have answered the questions? Would he have answered them truthfully? We will never know. Steinbeck was never asked to participate in such a study, and perhaps just as well. Often disagreeable, surly, touchy about personal matters, the burly novelist might have physically removed the interviewer, often a young female graduate student, from his doorstep.

However, we now have another source of information to turn to. The twenty questions can be addressed to the 1,116-page Benson biography. Here are the questions as they were worded in the NIMH study, and the answers they elicit from the biography.

1. *How old was Steinbeck the first time he ever drank enough to get drunk?*

Benson doesn't say but does mention that Steinbeck "learned to drink" at Stanford and had been "but an amateur at home" (p. 35). He also mentions that Steinbeck showed up at a Stanford football game with "row upon row of laboratory vials filled with grain alcohol . . . pinned neatly to the lining of his overcoat" (p. 41).

2. *Did Steinbeck's family ever object because he was drinking too much?*

Benson: "Before seeing his parents, John asked Lloyd [a friend] . . . not to mention anything concerning drinking" (p. 132). (This at least suggests some parental concern.)

Benson: ". . . Heavy drinking did exacerbate whatever strains there were in the relationship of Steinbeck and his wife. When he drank . . . he tended toward anger, becoming abusive and critical" (p. 355).

Benson: Steinbeck's mother-in-law thought he was "the most wicked man she had ever met," one reason being he associated with "ne'er-do-wells in bars" (p. 590).

Benson: "There were occasions when John would verbally abuse his wife in front of other people. . . . On one occasion . . . he and Carol went into town late in the evening to pick up some liquor, and Carol invited two deputy sheriffs whom they saw near the store to come back to their house with them" (pp. 415–16).

Benson: ". . . Mark and John were drinking together and . . . invented what they called the 'Aggressive Agreement'" about marriage. John mumbled, "'. . . you walk in and your wife says, "You're drunk." And you say, "You're damned right I am, and I'm going to get a lot drunker." And of course then she's got nothing to say'" (p. 787).

3. *Did Steinbeck ever think he was an excessive drinker?*

Steinbeck: "Last night when Carol called up she said her conscience was hurting her because she had done some bad things in a bar, so I said I had done a lot of bad things in bars . . ." (p. 463).

4. *Did Steinbeck ever drink as much as a fifth of liquor in a day—or three bottles of wine or as much as three six-packs of beer in one day?* (This indicates a high tolerance for alcohol and is included here in the problem category, since such consumption usually causes problems.)

Steinbeck: ". . . wine, beer and brandy ran like water. All evening. We toasted everything we could think of" (p. 356).

John's second wife: "John asked me to dance. He danced beautifully and tangoed very well, but . . . had been drinking all afternoon, and he went slow motion right over backward" (p. 462). The wife had to return to work and "left the men, still drinking."

Benson: ". . . John spent a good deal of time drinking Scotch with Ed, brooding . . ." (p. 566).

Benson: "On one occasion they went over, set up the electric train, and played with it while drinking gin and tonic until three in the morning" (p. 585).

Benson: "When they returned to pay the bill, they found that they had each consumed twenty-seven martinis the night before" (pp. 461–62). (This seems to clinch it.)

5. *Was there ever a period of two weeks when Steinbeck drank seven or more beers, seven or more drinks, or seven or more glasses of wine every day?*

Benson: "The Steinbecks went on to spend two weeks in New York, where they . . . went out on the town at every opportunity, returning to California . . . 'tired but happy . . . [saying,] I bet people are very glad to see us go after one of these splurges' " (p. 465).

6. *Was there ever a couple of months or more when Steinbeck drank that much—seven drinks, or seven bottles of beer, or seven glasses of wine—at least one evening a week?*

Benson doesn't say, but the answer almost certainly would be yes, as indicated by other information provided.

7. *Did friends, doctor, or clergyman ever tell Steinbeck he was drinking too much for his own good?*

Benson, citing a Steinbeck wife: ". . . he quarreled with every male friend he ever had and parted angrily from each of them" (p. 559). Elsewhere Benson said that Steinbeck was only rude when he drank (p. 354). Put these two facts together and you have the answer.

Benson: "After an evening of drinking, John made a pass at her, and she made it very clear that she didn't want to have any physical contact whatsoever . . . he hauled her to the second-story window of the bachelor quarters and, in a rage of drunken frustration, grabbed her by the ankles, hung her head down out the window, and began shaking her . . . Shebley spent several hours sobering up [Steinbeck] and telling him what an ass he was. Later that night, touched with remorse, Steinbeck realized that with one slip of the hand he could have killed the girl" (p. 137).

Benson: "Bert West . . . didn't like Steinbeck very much and thought of him as irresponsible ever since he caught him one evening lying in his bunk with a bottle of gin and shooting holes in the roof . . . with his revolver. He claimed to be ridding the place of packrats" (p. 141).

Benson: Steinbeck "went to Mexico, ostensibly to set up research [on a movie], but in reality to brawl and womanize his way through two long lost weekends. Alarmed that his friend might be slipping off the deep end, Pat Covici wrote to John in Cuernavaca . . .: 'I hope while you are in Mexico that you will do some tall thinking and wake up to yourself and your own peace of mind. It isn't simple, nor is it pleasant to look at the smashed pieces of something that you wanted to build and have. . . . It seems to me that a quick clean-up is the less painful, and a sober realization of what is sterling and what is not. . . .' After a week in New York again, he went back to Mexico . . . still drinking heavily . . ." (p. 618).

Benson doesn't say whether a clergyman or physician ever warned Steinbeck about his drinking, but he and his second wife got the minister who married them so drunk that he couldn't pronounce the words of the service (p. 516).

8. *Did Steinbeck ever want to stop drinking but couldn't?*

Benson: "They arrived at the restaurant about five and went into the bar for a drink before dinner. An hour later they were still drinking. . . . Four hours later the bartender had joined them . . . and they were surrounded by people, drinking and laughing. . . . Twice the manager came in to tell them the kitchen was closing. . . . Finally, a little after two in the morning, the bar closed [and they left]" (pp. 460–61).

9. *Some people promise themselves not to drink before five o'clock or never to drink alone, in order to control their drinking. Did Steinbeck ever do something like that?*

Benson: "His relationship with Goddard [Pauline] made all the gossip columns and it was widely reported that he was drinking heavily . . . even though he had stopped drinking entirely in January" (p. 631).

Benson: "He liked being with [a friend] so much that he didn't mind going without a drink during the conversation (when he wasn't going through one of his periods of 'not drinking' . . .)" (pp. 797–98). (People rarely stop drinking altogether unless there is a reason, and the most common reason is concern about a drinking problem.)

Benson: "The Steinbecks . . . had two months earlier given up drinking except on Saturday evenings and had substituted tea before dinner instead" (p. 787).

10. *Did Steinbeck ever have a drink before breakfast?*

Benson: "John and Carol's consumption of liquor increased, especially on weekends, when drinking sometimes began in the morning" (p. 416).

11. *Did Steinbeck ever have job or school troubles because of drinking on the job or at school?*

Benson: "[Steinbeck] had a pile of old gallon jugs, which he had collected for wine making . . . the wine making might have been a mistake . . . neither John nor the wine was able to work for very long" (p. 72).

Benson: "He told [an interviewer] that he gave up drinking while he was working on a book, and he told . . . others in letters during this period that he was not going out very much. Neither assertion is entirely accurate. The bar at home was open weekends, starting

Friday afternoon, and he did drink when he went out during the week, which was not uncommon" (p. 595).

Benson, quoting Burgess Meredith: " 'Getting out of himself' usually involved [John's] sitting around somewhere and drinking and talking. . . . 'I can see him sitting in "21" where he had his favorite table . . . glowing red like a ruby and with a high flush on his cheekbones . . . surrounding himself with his buddies' " (p. 595). (Steinbeck apparently missed a lot of work at his favorite table.)

Benson: "The two days of day and night partying at Louisville involved more drinking than they had done in a very long time, and John was pleased and surprised, since . . . one party usually disabled him for as much as two days afterward, that he was able to handle it" (p. 787).

12. *Did Steinbeck ever lose a job (or get kicked out of school) on account of drinking?*

No mention of it. But of course he was self-employed most of his adult life and attended college only when he felt like it.

13. *Did Steinbeck ever have trouble driving because of drinking?*

No mention of it.

14. *Was Steinbeck ever arrested because of drinking or for disturbing the peace while drinking?*

Benson, quoting Nathaniel Benchley: "Between 12:30 and 7 that evening, we had, each one, 14 [drinks]. . . . We kept calling our wives and saying, 'Don't worry. We'll be right home.' . . . There was somebody else at the bar who for some reason taunted John as being a cowboy, so John left him tied to the bar . . ." (p. 596). (Steinbeck *might* have been arrested, but apparently wasn't.)

15. *Did Steinbeck ever get into physical fights while drinking?*

A man had made a pass at Elaine at a party, half jokingly. Benson: "John, who was bent over slightly working at some project with his pocketknife, looked up and glared at the man. But the man continued his flirtation, and John said to him, 'Elaine is going to become my wife. I prefer that you don't do that.' Again, the man continued. John, very coldly and deliberately, stopped what he was doing, reached over the table with his knife, and dropped it, point down, onto the back of the man's hand, nicking the flesh" (p. 809). (If this *didn't* lead to a physical fight, it was probably because John was bigger and had the knife.)

16. *Did Steinbeck ever go on binges or benders, where he kept drinking for a couple of days or more without sobering up?*
Benson: "Steinbeck writes of a party . . . which lasted four days . . . [and] one that lasted two weeks, moving from house to house" (p. 228).
Benson: "The two days of day and night partying at Louisville involved more drinking than they had done in a very long time . . ." (p. 787).

17. *Did Steinbeck ever have blackouts while drinking—that is where he drank enough so that he couldn't remember what he had said or done?*
Benson: Steinbeck, after a night of drinking, "had signed into a hotel earlier that day using a pseudonym, and now that he was ready to go to bed, he couldn't remember what the pseudonym was and there weren't any other rooms available. He couldn't find Pare, because Pare was in another hotel and he couldn't remember which hotel" (p. 462).
Benson: "There was one late afternoon when he got out of '21' and caught a cab to go home. He settled back in his seat, and when the driver said 'Where to?' he replied, 'Murray Hill 4-3685.' The driver turned around and said, 'That's north, isn't it?' and John said, 'Yes,' not realizing what he had done until he had gotten all the way up to Ninetieth Street" (p. 595).
Benson: "When [Steinbeck, as a young man,] woke up [with a friend], somewhere in San Francisco, their heads hurt and they found that nearly all their money was gone" (p. 70). ("Somewhere in San Francisco" sounds very much like a blackout.)

18. *Did drinking ever cause Steinbeck to lose his ability to have sex relations so that he couldn't have sex even after sobering up?*
No mention of it.

19. *Did Steinbeck ever have symptoms of alcohol withdrawal (shakes, seizures, hallucinations, DTs)?*

Severe hangovers are mentioned on three occasions (pp. 605, 747, 777), but nothing worse.

20. *Did Steinbeck ever have a health problem from drinking (liver disease, stomach trouble, pancreatitis, tingling in the feet, or trouble with memory when not drinking)?*

Only one possible instance is mentioned.

Benson: "What was most frightening to him was that he was subject [when not drinking] to periodic blackouts and temporary loss of memory . . ." (p. 540). This followed a wartime accident in which an oil drum had "slammed against his head," and this may be the explanation—or it may not be.

Seventeen of the questions pertain to alcohol-related problems. Based purely on the content of Benson's biography, how many answers would the interviewer have scored as affirmative?

The information, of course, is grossly inadequate. A *real* interview would have included "probe" questions, such as "How many times, sir, did this happen?" "Did your mother-in-law oppose drinking on religious grounds?" "Did they arrest you for tying up that fellow in the bar?" A judgment would have been based on the *totality* of the answer, colored, no doubt, by a little unavoidable interview.bias. (Interviewers who drink tend to underscore; teetotalers overscore.)

Lacking the luxury of a relaxed two- or three-hour session with a cooperative subject, three research psychiatrists reviewed the "answers" in the book. Their opinions—whatever they may be worth— were unanimous.

Questions 2, 4, 7, 9, 10, 15, 16, and 17 indicated a problem.

Questions 3, 8, 11, and 14 suggested a problem, but more information was needed to be sure.

There is no information, one way or the other, pertaining to questions 12, 13, 18, 19, and 20. He may have had one or more of these problems but there is no way to tell. This also sometimes happens in real interviews. When it does, the item about which there is no information must be scored as negative—one of the rules of systematic interviewing.

How many alcohol-related problems are required to call a person "alcoholic"? Different scoring systems are employed by different investigators, a circumstance which leads to a good deal of confusion. This explains why quotation marks belong around the term "alcoholic" when referring to NIMH-type studies. Nevertheless, Steinbeck, based on this flimsiest of evidence, had eight problems. This would qualify him as "alcoholic" regardless of the scoring system used.

Can one trust Benson? There are two ways he could have erred: by overemphasizing a drinking problem or underemphasizing it.

There is no way to know whether he did either. However, on the subject of Steinbeck's drinking the book seems curiously evasive. From time to time Benson describes Steinbeck's getting drunk and hanging women by their feet out of windows or tying up men in bars, and then does not mention drinking again for fifty to a hundred pages. This may be a clue. Sherlock Holmes once solved a case by observing that a particular dog didn't bark. The same deductive logic could be applied to the Benson book. Sprinkled here and there are suggestions that Steinbeck was a boozer and a boozer with problems—and then the subject is dropped cold; years follow years and chapters follow chapters during which one would never suspect the fellow popped a single beer.

It *is* a bit reminiscent of Holmes's nonbarking dog. It would suggest Benson underemphasized Steinbeck's drinking problems.

Benson himself seems ambivalent about Steinbeck's drinking. He describes a Steinbeck who was frequently drunk and had social problems from drinking and at the same time he seems determined to convince the reader (and perhaps himself) that Steinbeck was not alcoholic. His explanation *why* he was not alcoholic is even more curious: Steinbeck wanted to avoid publicity.

> Steinbeck was inwardly and personally very conservative, and like so many middle-class Americans, his personal conservatism

was supported by an underlying puritanism that was exposed only when he was emotionally threatened or wounded. Anything extreme in his personal life threatened his privacy and the equilibrium that he felt he needed to function as a writer. *This is why he was rather more controlled in his drinking than many people thought he was and probably why, unlike many of his famous contemporaries, he never became an alcoholic.* He tended to put his writing in an Old Testament context; drinking and sex were temptations away from the purity of his goals. His worry about publicity was partly a moralistic worry about the damage that could be caused by pride. [Italics added.]

Yet, two paragraphs earlier Benson describes Steinbeck as "armed with a bottle of brandy" while holding a press conference, perhaps not the best way to avoid adverse publicity.

John Kenneth Galbraith also comes to Steinbeck's defense. In an article in the *Atlantic Monthly,* Galbraith tells about meeting John while vacationing on a Caribbean island:

It was . . . the beginning of a friendship. I can add little on Steinbeck as a writer, for he did not like talking about his work, at least to me. But I can tell quite a bit more about a shrewd and perceptive man, much interested in politics and contemporary anthropology and not only droll but very, very funny. He was a large man, still clean-shaven, exceedingly homely, and in 1954 looked older than I had imagined he was. He spoke in a carefully subdued mumble. . . .

John regularly took a mask and snorkel and, looking from shore like some terrible accident of marine miscegenation, went out along the reef to explore the underwater life.

(One can admire Steinbeck and still propose that Galbraith could write rings around him.)

Galbraith, Steinbeck, and their wives had drinks during cocktail hour. Galbraith called cocktail hour the Liberal Hour and Steinbeck called it the Milking Time. "Steinbeck," Galbraith observed, "differed from other novelists of his (or a slightly earlier) generation in being a controlled drinker. But he was also an appreciative one." During one Milking Time, Steinbeck told a bizarre story having, in Galbraith's opinion, "no appreciable relation to fact." Galbraith said it was "just as well that Hotchner was not around." Presumably he meant A.E. Hotchner, who had recently published a book exposing Hemingway's drunken behavior.

Often drunk but controlled: this appears to be the version of Steinbeck most favored by his friends and biographers. Galbraith's judgment may have been based largely on secondhand information. Although friends, they mainly corresponded and didn't see that much of each other.

Which should we believe: the friends or the NIMH research criteria? There are other definitions of alcoholism than the NIMH definition. How do *they* fit Steinbeck?

One is a definition proposed by the National Council on Alcoholism: "The person with alcoholism cannot consistently predict on any drinking occasion the duration of the episode or the quantity that will be consumed."

Does this describe Steinbeck? Benson reports that Steinbeck often abstained entirely from alcohol, although he disliked the term "going on the wagon." In the case of heavy drinkers, this is always suspicious. It suggests they may be more worried about alcohol than they let on—worried, perhaps, because they cannot "consistently predict" what will happen if they have a drink. Several times Benson suggests Steinbeck was indeed concerned about this and had reason for concern. A vow he took before traveling to Stockholm for the Nobel Prize can hardly be interpreted any other way:

> John had heard that the only American literature laureate who had gone to the ceremonies and remained sober was Pearl Buck . . . he was determined that his conduct would be flawless in this respect. (He also had been irritated that the old, false slander that he was an alcoholic had been intimated once again in the recent press attacks on him.) He knew from previous experience in Sweden what the rounds of parties and the constant toasting could do to even the most reserved of drinkers, and so he decided with Elaine [his wife] that they would not drink hard liquor during their stay, declining drink at the parties and accepting only wine at the dinners, where toasts would be offered. . . .
>
> That night in their hotel suite [after the ceremonies], John and Elaine packed and, for the first time, had drinks.

This is a vow no truly controlled drinker would ever take or need to take.

Finally, there is Charles Jackson's definition of alcoholism: "The alcoholic is a person who can take it or leave it, so he takes it." Jackson, an alcoholic and the author of *The Lost Weekend*, was talking about "denial," a cardinal feature of alcoholism.

"We are all victims of systematic self-deception," Santayana said, and the alcoholic is a victim par excellence. People are victims of many things—cancer, lust, society—and they can accept it. But, deep down, the alcoholic believes he is doing it to himself; he is the perpetrator, not the victim, and this he cannot accept, so he lies to himself:

"I can stop drinking any time. Important people drink. Churchill drank. Today is special—a friend is in town. Nothing is going on— why not? Life is tragic—why not? Tomorrow we die—why not?"

As he lies to himself, he lies to others, and concealment becomes a game like the one children play when they raid the cookie jar and hope their mother won't notice.

"Denial" and "rationalization" are the terms psychiatrists apply to the lies alcoholics tell themselves and others.

Like many writers, Steinbeck enjoyed telling lies. Perhaps among the lies were lies about his drinking. Perhaps the coverup goes on.

Perhaps.

Bibliographical Note

The principal source of data for this chapter was the mammoth biography of Steinbeck by Jackson J. Benson, *The True Adventures of John Steinbeck, Writer* (New York: Viking Press, 1984). Other biographies consulted were Peter Lisca's *The Wide World of John Steinbeck* (New Brunswick: Rutgers University Press, 1958) and Joseph Fontenrose's *John Steinbeck: An Introduction and Interpretation* (New York:

Holt, Rinehart, and Winston, 1963). The article by John Kenneth Galbraith describing his friendship with Steinbeck appeared in the November 1969 issue of *Atlantic Monthly*. A book written for high school and college teachers, *A Study Guide to Steinbeck* (Metuchen, N.J.: Scarecrow Press, 1974), describes his major works and provides a useful bibliography.

The interview used in this chapter is called the Diagnostic Interview Schedule (DIS) and was constructed by Drs. Lee Robins and John Helzer at Washington University in St. Louis in collaboration with Dr. Robert Spitzer at Columbia University. It was designed specifically for a large epidemiological survey of psychiatric illness and was sponsored by the National Institute of Mental Health. The first results of the survey were published in the October 1984 issue of *Archives of General Psychiatry*.

In May 1987 the American Psychiatric Association published the latest, most up-to-date criteria for alcoholism (called alcohol dependence by the APA). Nine manifestations were listed. If you had three, you were alcohol-dependent (that is, alcoholic). Not even Steinbeck's loyal biographer Benson could deny he had *three* of the following:

1. Alcohol often taken in larger amounts or over a longer period than the person intended;
2. Persistent desire or one or more unsuccessful efforts to cut down or control alcohol use;
3. A great deal of time spent in activities necessary to get alcohol, taking the substance, or recovering from its effects;
4. Frequent intoxication or withdrawal symptoms when expected to fulfill major role obligations at work, school, or home (e.g., does not go to work because hung over, goes to school or work intoxicated, or intoxicated while taking care of his or her children), or when alcohol use is physically hazardous (e.g., drives when intoxicated);
5. Important social, occupational, or recreational activities given up or reduced because of alcohol;
6. Continued alcohol use despite knowledge of having a persistent or recurrent social, psychological, or physical problem that is caused or exacerbated by the use of the substance;
7. Marked tolerance: need for markedly increased amounts of the substance (i.e., at least a 50% increase) in order to achieve

intoxication or desired effect, or markedly diminished effect with
continued use of the same amount;
8. Characteristic withdrawal symptoms;
9. Alcohol often taken to relieve or avoid withdrawal
symptoms.*

*From *Diagnostic and Statistical Manual of Mental Disorders*, 3d ed. rev. (Washington,
D.C.: The American Psychiatric Association, 1987).

5

SIMENON
Learning to Drink American-Style

*From one end of the country to the other there exists a
freemasonry of alcoholics. . . .*

Simenon

Patterns of drinking are variable and it is a mistake to associate one
particular pattern exclusively with alcoholism. America's best-
known authority on alcoholism, E.M. Jellinek, divided alcoholics
into various "species," depending on their pattern of drinking. One
species, the gamma alcoholic, is common in America and conforms
to the stereotype of the Alcoholics Anonymous alcoholic. Gamma
alcoholics have problems with "control." Once they begin drinking,
they are unable to stop until poor health or depleted financial re-
sources prevent them from continuing. Once the bender is terminated, however, the person is able to abstain from alcohol for vary-
ing lengths of time.

Jellinek contrasted the gamma alcoholic with a species of alcoholic common in France. The latter has control but is "unable to
abstain"; he *must* drink a given quantity of alcohol every day, although he has no compulsion to exceed this amount. He may not
recognize that he has an alcohol problem until, for reasons beyond
his power, he has to stop drinking, whereupon he experiences
withdrawal symptoms.

A French alcoholic describes himself:

My name is Pierre. I am not an alcoholic. I do not know alcoholics. There are no alcoholics in France, except tourists.

I have drunk wine since I was a child. Wine is good for you. I
drink it with meals and when I am thirsty. Since I was a young
man, I have drunk three or four liters of wine every day. I also

enjoy an occasional apéritif, especially on Sunday mornings and after work. I never drink more than this. I have no problems from alcohol.

Once, when I was in the Army, no wine was permitted. I started shaking all over and thought bugs were crawling on me. I think it was the Army food. My doctor says my liver is too large. My father and grandfather had large livers. It probably means nothing.

The American alcoholic stereotype has two choices—abstain or go on a bender. The French alcoholic stereotype does not go on benders, but cannot abstain.

Georges Simenon had the not very enviable distinction of being both a French-type and an American-type alcoholic, switching from the former to the latter in middle age. The Belgian-born novelist has some interesting things to say about alcoholism in America and how he caught the bug. Simenon's story shows the influence of culture on the drinking of a drinking writer.

Simenon started keeping notebooks when he was nearing sixty and feeling depressed. The notebooks were published ten years later under the title *When I Was Old*. By this time he had stopped feeling depressed and stopped keeping notebooks. It is too bad about the notebooks. They are full of information about writing. They also tell a lot about drinking. Simenon had vast experience with both.

Simenon may be the world's greatest underappreciated writer. Some European critics believe he deserves the Nobel Prize. Most Americans think of him as a detective story writer, the creator of Inspector Maigret. This is not fair. Less than half of his several hundred novels are about Maigret, and the best "Maigrets" are superb novels, not who-done-its at all. John Raymond, a literary critic for the *Times* (London), calls Simenon (now retired) the greatest storyteller of our day. Gide, Hemingway, and other famous writers have praised him extravagantly. Because Simenon is popular, rich, and easy to read, however, his stock among the literati has generally not been high.

Maybe it will rise as word gets around about his "drinking problem." As Leslie Fiedler said, every writer, really to be admired, needs a "charismatic flaw." Drunkenness appears to be the flaw most admired by Americans.

For many years—roughly from 1935 to 1949—writing and drinking were inseparable for Simenon. In *When I Was Old*, he discusses how the drinking began and how it ended. The subject also comes up in his tasteless memoir of un-Simenon length published in English translation in 1984. Some years ago I had an opportunity to spend an afternoon with Simenon discussing his work and thoughts about drinking. Putting together these sources, the following story emerges:

"There will be legends about this too," Simenon wrote.

> Certain people have seen me working on red wine, others on cider, on muscatel, on whiskey, on grog, I don't know what else, and for each it is an eternal verity. Those who have seen me drunk will always see me as drunk, and the contrary is also true.
>
> Of all the dangers I have run . . . this [alcoholism] is undoubtedly the most serious. It preoccupied me so much that I have studied the question as only specialists have done . . . I could fill a notebook with statistics.

As a child in Liège, Belgium, Simenon was repeatedly warned about the dangers of drink; there was no wine or liquor in the house. The words "He drinks" were uttered with consternation, especially by the mother. Her father, brother, and two sisters were alcoholics.

Simenon had his first drink at fourteen, eau de vie used to seal jars with waxed paper. It made him feel good and he tried it again, replacing what he drank with water. Soon there was nothing but water in the decanter. For a long time it was believed the alcohol content had evaporated. Simenon minimized the importance of this experience while granting the "attraction of forbidden fruit."

Subsequently, he did little drinking until his twenties in Paris. There, as a reporter and budding novelist, he drank because it was the fashion: "All of the painters of the period were heavy drinkers, while the American novelists were even more so." Steadily, however, his consumption of wine increased. While traveling along the canals in France, writing Maigret stories, he used to fill a ten-liter demijohn with wine at pumps that "looked like gas pumps." Nevertheless, at the time, "I drank when I was thirsty, never to get drunk." Somewhat later, however, literary inspiration as well as thirst prompted drinking: "I got the habit of working on wine." Starting at six in the morning, he drank and wrote throughout the day.

From the mid-1930s until 1945, "the habit was formed . . . white wine at Concarneau (cider in the afternoon), red in Paris or elsewhere, grog when I had a cold, brandy and water at other times." Simenon says he rarely got drunk but

> needed, as early as the morning, especially to write, a pick-me-up. I was persuaded in good faith that it was impossible to write otherwise. And, away from work, I drank anything, apéritif, cognac, calvados, marc, champagne. . . .
>
> I was not at all aware of being an alcoholic, but only a temperamental fellow. . . . I traveled a lot and while traveling I drank more.

Simenon spent the war in occupied France, then in 1945 came to the United States where he drank "American-style": "no longer wine with my meals, but before them, Manhattan after Manhattan, then dry martini after dry martini. . . ."

With this came "painful awakenings, hangovers, attacks of gas pains during which I thought I was dying of angina pectoris."

In this period Simenon married his second wife and "we had two or three months of wild life." Eventually, however, she persuaded him to try writing without alcohol. To see if it could be done, they went to a snowbound cabin in New England where, "trembling," his wife waited behind the door of his study, "listening to the rhythm of the typewriter, and ceaselessly bringing me hot tea. I left the door half open, stuck my hand out and grabbed the cup without a word. . . . I was sure I would never come to the end of that book."

His wife had reason to tremble, for if the experiment had failed, Simenon said, he would, in all probability, never have tried it again, and "I would be dead at this moment." The experiment didn't fail. The book that resulted, *Three Beds in Manhattan*, is one of Simenon's best.

Afterward, the Simenons continued to drink "pretty seriously" from time to time, then "cut the liquor, allowing ourselves only beer. . . . Finally, one fine day we decided to put ourselves on the wagon . . . not out of virtue, only because we knew that we were, both of us, incapable of stopping in time."

This was in 1949. Afterward, on occasion, they drank alcohol for two or three days "out of hygiene," so it would not "seem a deprivation, thus an obsession." Other times they drank Coca-Cola.

At the time he wrote the above, in 1961, Simenon still considered himself an alcoholic. "Few of my French friends understand it. And I resent those who have made drink the indispensable complement to every friendly, worldly, or even official meeting."

When I saw him years later, in his home near Lausanne, Switzerland, he was drinking tea (while pouring Scotch for his guest with a heavy hand). He said alcohol was no longer a problem. He had a drink now and then, especially in airports because he was afraid of flying. He looked ten years younger than his sixty-nine years: a bustling, animated, friendly man who likes doctors and may know more medicine than most. (A less attractive Simenon comes over in *Intimate Memoirs*, published in his eighties, but perhaps age explains it.)

Simenon believed that alcohol would kill him but that he could not write without it. It turned out he could. In neither quantity nor quality did his work suffer from abstinence. If alcohol was his muse, it was a dispensable muse.

Simenon has this to say about drinking in America:

> . . . I did not become truly alcoholic with an alcoholic consciousness except in America. . . .
>
> I'm speaking of a particular, almost permanent state, in which one is dominated by alcohol, whether during the hours one is drinking or during the hours when one is impatiently waiting to drink, almost as painfully as a drug addict waits for his injection.
>
> If one has never known this experience, it is difficult to understand American life. Not that everyone drinks, in the sense in which my mother used the word, but because it is part of private and public life, of folklore, you might say, as is proved by the large, more or less untranslatable vocabulary, most often in slang, that relates to drink. . . .
>
> All of life is colored by it. New York, for example, seems made to be seen in this state, and then it is an extraordinary New York and, strange as it may seem, comradely.

The crowds cease to be anonymous, the bars cease to be ordinary ill-lit places, the taxi drivers complaining or menacing people. It is the same for all the big American cities. Los Angeles, San Francisco, Boston. . . . From one end of the country to the other there exists a freemasonry of alcoholics. . . .

Simenon says that for twenty years in France he drank without remorse, without seeing anything wrong with it. "In the United States I learned shame. For they are ashamed. Everyone is ashamed. I was ashamed like the rest."

In my conversation with Simenon, he said that alcoholism was less common among French writers than among American writers, and ventured a possible reason: "Americans must experience what they write about. French writers work within a tradition."

Unlike a traditionalist such as Anatole France, whose work is elegant and reassuring, Simenon writes from personal experience, is rarely elegant, and almost never reassuring. He writes about people, places, and weather he has known, beginning in the reverse order.

"I first find some atmosphere. Today there is a little sunshine here. I might remember such and such a spring, maybe in some small Italian town, or some place in the French provinces or in Arizona, and then, little by little, a small world will come into my mind, with a few characters."

And somewhere in every Simenon novel is a problem that has worried him personally. "I know that there are many men who have more or less the same problems I have, with more or less intensity, and who will be happy to read the book to find the answer—if the answer can be found."

Simenon apparently found an answer to his drinking problem. Nowhere in his several hundred novels does he tell, alas, how it was done.

Bibliographical Note

Simenon's book *When I Was Old* (New York: Harcourt Brace Jovanovich, 1971) cannot be recommended too highly for anyone interested in writers and how they live and work.

Less recommended is Simenon's autobiographical *Intimate Memoirs* (New York: Harcourt Brace Jovanovich, 1984), an unfortunate book about, among other things, his daughter's suicide.

Fenton Bresler's *The Mystery of Georges Simenon* (New York: Beaufort, 1983) is the best book about Simenon's life and work available in English.

Pierre's story, at the beginning, was taken from my book *Is Alcoholism Hereditary?* (New York: Ballantine, 1988).

The evidence that 1949 was the exact year when Simenon achieved permanent sobriety is somewhat contradictory. In the biography by Bresler, Simenon's son, John, relates that, even after 1949, ". . . he would mostly start after lunch and then it would build up. There would be times when he was not drinking for as long as two months, but then I would come back from school in the afternoon and find him not himself. I have memories of specific scenes—and of my father being very drunk and throwing glasses and my mother having hysterics." It is not clear in what years this occurred, but the bulk of the evidence indicates that Simenon's drinking decreased sharply in his fifties. In his eighties he was looking fit and healthy and showed no physical signs of alcoholism.

6

FAULKNER
The Count No'Count Who Went to Stockholm

There is a lot of nourishment in an acre of corn.

Faulkner

Most people today are probably unaware that William Clark Faulkner wrote most of his novels at night while his faithful servant Nathan whisked away the flies and supplied him with the bourbon whiskey which he consumed in large amounts. Faulkner often worked well past midnight and then, to relax, bowled for a half hour or so on the alley he had set up in his front yard, with Nathan as pin boy.

During the daytime Faulkner ran the railroad he had built linking Ripley, Mississippi, with Middleton, Tennessee. It was twenty-four miles long and had two trains. Most people probably aren't aware of this either.

Faulkner's best-known book was *The White Rose of Memphis*, a melodramatic novel that became one of the great popular successes of its era: it sold one hundred sixty thousand copies and ran through thirty-five editions. *It was published in 1880.*

William Clark Faulkner's great-grandson, William *Cuthbert* Faulkner, asked by his third grade teacher what he wanted to be when he grew up, said, "I want to be a writer like my great-granddaddy." The boy got his wish.

William Clark Faulkner was a Civil War colonel who fought in the first battle of Bull Run. He was a brutal man with his troops and they fired him (you could do this in the Civil War). He later became one of Mississippi's most distinguished citizens. He not only built a railroad and wrote books but also built a prosperous law practice and was successful in politics.

He also drank a lot and killed a couple of fellow citizens. Then his partner killed him. Today there is in the Ripley, Mississippi, cemetery a statue of Colonel Faulkner, a small, ferocious-looking man.

You will find Colonel Faulkner in many of his great-grandson's books. His fictional name is John Sartoris. In the books Sartoris has a son modeled after Colonel Faulkner's son, who was nicknamed the Little Colonel. The Little Colonel was also distinguished. He was college-educated, a prosperous lawyer, president of the First National Bank in Oxford. He also drank a lot. Nearly every year he would order his bags packed, mount his fine carriage, and be driven off by his Negro servant, Ned, to the Keeley Institute for the "cure."

He had a son named Murry. The son was not as successful as the old colonel and the young colonel, but he had one thing in common with them: he drank a lot. He, too, made frequent trips to Memphis to take the Keeley Cure.

Murry had four sons. The eldest, William, considered by many to be America's greatest writer, was a heavy drinker from adolescence until the day he died. Another son, John, also a writer, was a heavy drinker. A third son, Jack, an FBI agent, finally had to join Alcoholics Anonymous because of his drinking. The fourth and youngest son, Dean, liked to drink but died in his twenties before it might have gotten out of hand.

Estelle, William's wife, also was alcoholic and joined AA but this was well into the twentieth century and she was the first Faulkner woman to drink at all. William's mother, Maud, used to pour his liquor down the kitchen sink and ask him why he drank so much, and he said he didn't know, but she never really came down hard on him or on her other sons. The women were generally tolerant of the men's drinking.

Jack Falkner (most of the family left the *u* out of their name) described how it was.

Back in the good old days, at least in our part of the country, liquor was an accepted way of life as far as many of the menfolk were concerned. Few women would touch it on pain of certain and universal condemnation by the community. This did not mean that men were taught to indulge in it, anymore than they were instructed to rise when a lady entered a room, to lie only when it would be of great value to another, or to take pride in their family and their country. These things—the drinking, the code of personal conduct and philosophy of life—were simply passed on from generation to generation by manners and deportment, no succeeding one having sought or found a more agreeable way to live with his fellows.

Mother detested whiskey, and it was forever beyond her understanding how a man could bring himself to partake voluntarily of something which contrived only to make him a bigger fool than nature had done in the first place. Unfortunately, this did not deter our father anymore than it did most of the rest of us in later life.

Obviously Jack could turn a phrase. Writing talent, like alcoholism, runs in families.

William Faulkner (dropping the Cuthbert) was born in 1897. He was a colicky baby, but any connection between colic and winning the Nobel Prize (or drinking a lot) is undemonstrated. As a boy growing up in a small college town in the early part of the century, William seemed no different from any other barefoot boy who stayed more or less out of trouble and did pretty well in school. Looking back, family and neighbors would note that he had a lot of imagination but whether they would have noted it at the time is not certain. Like his mother, he had a flair for drawing and painting and some of his pen-and-ink drawings in his teens were almost professional. He was surrounded by gifted storytellers, particularly his black mammy and his grandfather, the banker. His grandfather talked much of the Civil War and the flamboyant Colonel Faulkner who fought in it. He often drank whiskey while telling the stories and let Billy finish off what was left in the glass. This is probably William's first experience with alcohol and nothing in the records suggests he spat out the vile-tasting brew. Hanging around his father's livery stable, he came to love horses like all the Faulkner males and went hunting and fishing at every opportunity. His mother introduced him to the world of literature. She read as voraciously as the men in the family drank.

Sometime in his early teens Faulkner changed. He lost interest in school and his grades dropped. He became shy and withdrawn. He spent long hours sitting around the courthouse square just staring at people. The famous taciturnity—Faulkner's most pronounced personality trait—became established. He showed an early gift for making up stories and kept the other kids spellbound, but he told them fewer and fewer tales. He started writing poetry.

Faulkner always thought of himself as mainly a poet. When he started writing fiction he did so hoping to make a little money so he could afford to write poetry. Even when he came to recognize that his poetry would never be better than second- or third-rate, he still wrote poems and had them published privately. It was through his poetry that Faulkner came to know a country lawyer named Phil Stone, who was undoubtedly the greatest influence in his life.

Stone was a brilliant, erudite, Yale-educated lawyer of the type common in small towns, wise, talkative, highly educated, and out of place among the farmers and storekeepers who had had little schooling and never read books. As a teenager, Faulkner happened to show Stone some of his poems. Stone saw the talent. For many years he served as a private tutor for Faulkner, telling him whom to read, what to write, and where to send his poems. Stone was Faulkner's college education. Bill lost all interest in school and stopped attending classes. He sat around the square or in his father's hardware store, with his feet propped up, distant and dreamy. But he saw a lot of Stone. In later years, after Faulkner became world-famous and put Oxford on the map, Stone would see little of *him*. The reason isn't clear, but Faulkner had a habit of turning on people who befriended him and he had apparently offended his mentor. The same thing happened with Sherwood Anderson, who, some years later, became his friend and mentor in New Orleans and helped him get his first novel published. Faulkner wrote savage caricatures of Anderson and Anderson never forgave him.

It is not clear how Faulkner got along financially during the time when he stopped being a schoolboy and his first literary success at thirty-four. There was some money in the family—his grandfather, after all, was a bank president—but Murry, William's father, was a failure in business and ended up as a low-salaried alumni secretary at the University of Mississippi, where the family lived in a house on the campus. William was considered lazy. "He just *wouldn't* work," his Uncle John recalled. In school he gazed out the window and answered the simplest question with "I don't know." He worked for a time as a bookkeeper and then in his grandfather's bank where he had access to store-bought whiskey. Mostly he wrote poems and stories and drew pictures, sometimes illustrating his own poems and stories.

His dress was unpredictable. For a time he dressed like a dandy, knotting rich silk ties beneath high starched white collars, combing his hair in a pompadourlike style. It is not clear where he got the money for the clothes, but it was probably from his mother, who still treated the family as aristocracy. Most of the time his dress was non-descript: baggy pants, frayed collars, mismatched shoes. In his late teens he started visiting Memphis, some one hundred miles north of Oxford, where he sampled the prostitutes, drank, and gambled. It is not clear where he got the money for these things, either.

Then came World War I. Rejected by the U.S. military because of his size (five feet six inches), he joined the Royal Air Force in Canada, lying about his nationality. Just before receiving his commission the war ended. For years afterward he dressed up in his RAF uniform on Armistice Day and told brazen lies about having combat experience in France and crashing his plane.

He may indeed have crashed his plane. As related in his book, his brother Jack once asked if he had had a crackup.

"Yes," he said. "The war quit on us before we could do anything about it. The same day they lined up the class, thanked us warmly, and announced that we would be discharged the next day, which meant that we had the afternoon to celebrate the Armistice and some airplanes to use in doing it. I took up a rotary-motored Spad with a crock of bourbon in the cockpit, gave diligent attention to both, and executed some reasonably adroit chandelles, an Immel-mann or two, and part of what could easily have turned out to be a nearly perfect loop."

"What do you mean—part of a loop?" Jack asked.

William chuckled. "That's what it was; a hangar got in the way and I flew through the roof and ended up hanging on the rafters."

This may not have been true either. Faulkner was a prodigious liar. In later life when he became a famous novelist he had to remove references to his combat experience from the dust jackets of his books, an embarrassment. At any rate, like his three brothers, he loved flying and eventually bought an airplane. Again, it is not clear where he got the money. His youngest brother, Dean, took paying passengers up in the plane and had a fatal crash.

After the war Faulkner entered the University of Mississippi as a special student but this didn't last long. He spent some time in Greenwich Village and the French Quarter in New Orleans, sharing apartments and drinking cheap booze, but it is unclear how he could afford even this. His writing was bringing in almost no money. In his early twenties, he sold a poem to the *New Republic* for $15, but his other writings were rejected by everyone except college newspapers and the *Times-Picayune* (New Orleans), which ran a series of Faulkner sketches. His first novel, *Soldiers' Pay*, got some good reviews but sold few copies. Nevertheless, he spent six months in Europe and did so without starving in a garret. Perhaps his mother helped.

At Ole Miss he did hold one job that did nothing to change his reputation as a worthless fellow. For several months Faulkner was postmaster of the branch at the university. He was not a success. The mail piled up, the hours of opening were vague, the records confused, the customers' complaints met with silence or abuse—while Faulkner drank, wrote poetry, and took long walks. Before he could be fired, he quit, saying he never again would be at the "beck and call of every son-of-a-bitch who had two cents for a postage stamp."

Anyway he received a salary and people now understood how he could afford fancy clothes when he felt in the mood to wear them (when he wore them, the townfolk called him Count No'Count).

At thirty-two he married Estelle Franklin, his childhood sweetheart, borrowing money for the honeymoon. This may have provided some financial relief. Estelle was receiving alimony and child support for two children by a former marriage. However, the marriage was rocky from the beginning. Angry that Estelle was an alcoholic—as Faulkner himself was—he also complained that she "never had any regard or respect for my work, has always looked on it as a hobby, like collecting stamps." He felt bored, fed up, in a marriage with a family that seemed a constant drain on his finances and emotions. However, they had a daughter, Jill, whom he adored and he never made the break with Estelle because he acknowledged "a responsibility to the female child whose presence in the world I am accountable for."

From time to time Estelle also considered divorce, partly because she recognized that her husband was "frightfully unhappy." She also resented his "compulsion to be attached to some young woman at all times" and she was outraged when he brought one of his protégées into their house and made their daughter aware of his infidelities. Without Bill and Jill, however, Estelle said she would be a "nonentity." The two stayed married until Faulkner's death at sixty-five.

By his early thirties Faulkner had written three novels. Some got favorable reviews but none sold well. Then, deliberately, he wrote a novel conceived to make money. Based on a "cheap idea" much denigrated by its author, *Sanctuary,* published when Faulkner was thirty-four, was a huge popular success. It was made into a movie and now, for the first time, Faulkner could afford more than fancy clothes. He took some of the money and bought a rundown pre–Civil War house on the edge of town which, over the next thirty years, he gradually restored into a handsome, comfortable home. After *Sanctuary,* however, his books still sold poorly. Faulkner finally succumbed to a temptation that had been the downfall and despair of other depression-times gifted writers: Hollywood.

In 1932 Faulkner boarded a train for Hollywood and went to work for Metro-Goldwyn-Mayer. Faulkner recalled that he was scared by the hullabaloo over his arrival and got flustered and then drunk. For the next dozen years Faulkner traveled back and forth from Hollywood to Oxford. He invariably reached his destination intoxicated.

While working for the studios—first Metro-Goldwyn-Mayer, then Twentieth Century–Fox, and later Warner Brothers—he wrote numerous screenplays and assisted on others. He received little recognition and his salary fluctuated from $500 to $1,000 a week to nothing. His contract said he would be automatically terminated if he drank on the lot. He drank a good deal on the lot, as well as elsewhere, and from time to time was blackballed. When too drunk to write, he sometimes dictated. He met in Hollywood a young woman who became his off-and-on mistress for the next fifteen years. He drank with Bogart and Gable. He did the screenplay for Hemingway's *To Have and Have Not*, one of the few times he received a screen credit.

In Hollywood he continued to write novels, rising early in the morning to work on one or to write a short story before going to the studio. His novels were serious; the short stories tended to be, in his words, trash. Faulkner's inability to make a living as a serious novelist reduced him, like Fitzgerald, to writing commercial stories that sometimes appeared in the *Saturday Evening Post* and other national magazines but that mostly were rejected. Robert Graves once said that he wrote fiction to have money to write poetry, which he compared to raising chickens to afford a cat. It was the same with William Faulkner.

During Faulkner's Hollywood years his literary stock fell steadily. What recognition he received was mostly from foreign writers and critics, some of whom made treks to Oxford, which both annoyed and amused Faulkner's neighbors. To them he was still Count No'Count.

By the early forties all of Faulkner's books were out of print and the copper type plates had been sold for the war effort. Then, in the middle forties, a Faulkner revival began which, in the next ten years, brought him virtually every literary award the world had to offer.

He was first discovered by Europeans, particularly Arnold Bennett in England and Jean-Paul Sartre in France. The French had a knack for discovering American literary geniuses. Poe had had the same fate—scorned and rejected in his own country and idolized in France. The critic Malcolm Cowley was probably as responsible for the Faulkner revival as anyone else. In 1946 he brought out a collection of Faulkner's works for the Viking Portable Library series. Cowley told Faulkner about a conversation he had had with Jean-Paul Sartre. "Pour les Jeunes en France, Faulkner c'est un dieu," Sartre had said. Albert Camus went further, calling Faulkner the greatest writer in the world. By the time Faulkner was forty-eight, the attention had got him on the cover of *Time*, which compared him to Shakespeare.

His reviews at home, however, were still mixed and often bad. "The world of William Faulkner," wrote Granville Hick, "echoes with a hideous trampling march of lust and disease, brutality and death." Other critics found Faulkner unreadable. One accused him of writing while in delirium tremens. (Once or twice, it may have been true.) The top American writers—Hemingway, Anderson, Fitzgerald, O'Hara, and others—gave Faulkner high ratings. Hemingway, in a drunken conversation, insisted that Faulkner was better than he was. Faulkner, he said, had the most talent of them all. "I would have been happy just to have managed him." Characteristically, Hemingway later took some of it back. He conceded that Faulkner had abundant natural gifts but said he had written too much and wrote when he was tired, "sometimes going on alcohol," adulterating the works with "tricks" and "rhetoric."

John O'Hara, on the other hand, called Faulkner "our only living genius." Indeed, of all the twentieth-century American writers, Faulkner had the adjective *genius* attached to his name more often than anyone else. He called himself, at least once, a "prodigious" genius. Edmund Wilson called him a genius, and Wilson did not say these things lightly.

During his thirties and forties, Faulkner met and drank with nearly all of the well-known writers: Lewis, Dreiser, Mencken, Dorothy Parker, the New York literary crowd in general. He and Dashiell Hammett often passed out simultaneously. Mencken could keep up with his drinking but only if they both drank beer. They all expressed great admiration for Faulkner, and although the critics kept sniping and carping, the American writers and the literati in Europe agreed that Faulkner was the best there was.

His neighbors didn't share this feeling. The *Oxford Eagle* reported the reaction of most of his fellow townsmen: "Mr. Faulkner, a great writer? Well, they sure wouldn't hire him to write a Chamber of Commerce booklet for the town." While visitors poured into Oxford to see the great man sitting on his porch drinking whiskey, neighbors said, "We don't want to talk about him." Commenting on the apathy and hostility at home, Faulkner said he was like the hound dog that stays under a country wagon on the square. "He might be cajoled or scared out for a short distance, but first thing you know he has scuttled back under the wagon."

Faulkner might have been a hound in Oxford but in the literary capitals of the world he was a lion. In 1949 he received the highest honor the world has to offer a writer: the Nobel Prize in literature.

When Faulkner learned about the prize, he first said he had no intention of going to Stockholm. Then he was prevailed upon by his daughter, Jill, to go and reluctantly made plans to take the trip. But first, for a period of a few days, he got completely drunk. Hoping to get him stopped early enough to be in shape for the trip, the family crossed off on the calendar several days that had not arrived yet. Faulkner caught on and said with relief, "Ah, I can drink for three more days." He sobered up a day or so before flying to Stockholm, arriving sober but unshaven and in a bad mood. He gave an eloquent acceptance talk and then promptly got drunk.

Back home neighbors didn't know what to do about their celebrity. The Nobel Prize was too important to ignore. Something had to be done. Finally, they had a fish fry and invited Faulkner as the honored guest. He accepted.

After winning the Nobel Prize and later becoming an officer of the French Legion of Honor, as well as picking up a Pulitzer Prize and other awards, Faulkner just kept on writing books. He valued his privacy more than ever and refused interviews or any other public attention. *Time* wanted him on its cover again and he said no. President Kennedy invited him to the White House and he said it was too far to go "for a dinner with strangers." He was pestered so much by tourists and carloads of English majors that he dug deep ruts in his cedar-lined drive to his antebellum home, but this didn't stop people from coming up to the porch and into the house, sometimes taking away souvenirs like an ashtray or a swizzle stick.

After his daughter married a young West Pointer and moved with him to Charlottesville, Virginia, Faulkner was lured to Charlottesville to become a resident-in-writing at the University of Virginia. While there he became friends with Joseph Blotner, who later was a pallbearer at his funeral, and still later produced a definitive two-volume biography of Faulkner. While in Virginia Faulkner took up with the fox-hunting set and rode to the hounds dressed in a pink coat, a bowler hat, and a flask in his pocket. He decided he would like to live in or near Charlottesville and he and Estelle looked for a house to buy. Before they could make the move, Faulkner got drunk and checked into a sanitarium near Oxford where, at 1:30 A.M. on July 6, 1962, he died of a heart attack.

By the time of his death even the reddest necked Oxonians had acquired a grudging regard for the writer, thanks to his book *Intruder in the Dust*. It was filmed in Oxford, with the mayor and other citizens as extras, and there premièred. His neighbors went to the funeral, but were outnumbered by reporters and photographers, who came from around the world to report the death of "America's greatest writer."

Faulkner was not a religious man, although he never rejected the possibility that God might exist (as had Sartre and other existentialists who admired him). He sometimes went to church but with little enthusiasm. Chatting with his brother Jack outside the funeral home following his mother's death, Faulkner told him that his idea of immortality was that each of them would become something like a radio wave.

What kind of man was Faulkner? There are many descriptions of his physical appearance but the best is by Robert Coughlan, who interviewed Faulkner against his wishes, and wrote for *Life* magazine a two-part series that was so well written that even Faulkner might have forgiven him if Faulkner had read it (Faulkner never read about himself, nor even his novels after he finished them).

Coughlan described Faulkner as follows:

> William Faulkner is a small, wiry man of 56 with close-cropped iron-gray hair, an upswept mustache of a darker color, thin, high-bridged aquiline nose, heavy-lidded and deeply set brown eyes in which melancholy, calculation and humor are variously reflected, and a face tanned and webbed, especially near the eyes with the creases and lines and tiny tracings of advancing middle-age and the erosion of many days spent in the open in all weather. He is entirely self-possessed, with a manner easy, courteous, speculative and deadly. He is a quiet man, yet when he is at ease, with his short legs outstretched and a blackened pipe in his thin mouth and perhaps a drink at his elbow, he is like a somnolent cat but still in the wink of an eye could kill a mouse. Faulkner does not look or act like what he is. He acts like a farmer who has studied Plato and looks like a river gambler.

In short, Faulkner had a mixture of traits, good and bad. Perhaps the most attractive aspect of his personality showed in his behavior toward his daughter, Jill, and two stepchildren. Jill said it could be wonderful being with him, just doing simple things. Faulkner took the children on hayrides, and after they built a bonfire out in the country he would tell stories and lead them in songs like "Old Mac-Donald Had a Farm." At other times he might lead a horseback-riding group of Jill and five or six others, setting out along a favorite trail. (Jill was a close friend of Joseph Blotner, the official Faulkner biographer, and his books are full of such detail.) Dad sometimes took Jill to the carnival and to mystery films, mimicking the actors they had seen on screen. Faulkner reminds one of Fitzgerald in this regard. Fitzgerald also had an only child, Scotty, whom he adored.

But for neither Jill Faulkner nor Scotty Fitzgerald was Life with Father a bed of roses.

They both had closeup views of their fathers' alcoholism. Jill appealed to Faulkner to stop drinking. "Think of me," she pleaded. But it was too late, and he answered with a phrase she never forgot: "Nobody remembers Shakespeare's children." Sometimes she helped him into bed. Once he toppled down the staircase. Once, she having invited friends to visit, her father and mother were both drinking when they arrived. "It was horribly embarrassing," she recalls, but there was nothing she felt she could do except sit there, seething.

Faulkner's relationship with others in the family was generally good. He got along poorly with his father but was close to his mother, whom he visited daily when in Oxford. He was at least pleasant and sometimes generous to all of the brothers, uncles, cousins, and in-laws in Oxford and environs.

Many of them appeared in his books, for which not many were grateful. He lent probably more money than he borrowed, which may explain why he stayed mostly broke even after his books were reissued, became popular, and were made into movies.

It is incredible that Faulkner survived to be nearly sixty-five. He lived in the romantic tradition—recklessly. As an RAF pilot (if you believe him), he crashed his plane into a hangar to "celebrate the

Armistice." He rode horses like a maniac, riding with his stirrups too long and his toes pointed out, taking the jumps with his knees out instead of tight to his mount. He fell off repeatedly, fracturing vertebrae and collarbones and getting concussions.

But his most reckless behavior was his drinking. He drank from early adolescence to the day before his death. He liked Old Crow, Jack Daniels, anything with corn in it ("There is a lot of nourishment in an acre of corn," he said), but he would drink anything (absinthe in Paris, ouzo in Greece, moonshine in Oxford). As mentioned, his grandfather and father regularly took the Keeley Cure for alcoholism and abstained for various periods. His wife and brother Jack joined Alcoholics Anonymous, with success. But, except for the brief periods of voluntary abstinence ("so it won't become a habit") and the many times he went to a hospital to dry out, Faulkner drank daily and, frequently, ferociously.

His policy toward drinking was as follows:

1. Have whiskey available at all times (he was rarely without a pocket flask).

2. As a rule, don't drink until sunset—and then have only a few (consistent with getting up early the next day to write masterpieces).

3. Sometimes have more than a few—what the hell, life is short; the writer has a cold or a toothache or pain from falling off a horse; or a story is rejected; or his latest love loves him not back; or it's a gray day; or it's New York and everybody gets drunk in New York. Faulkner always had reasons for getting potted. His recuperative powers were legendary; after a few days in a hospital or tapering off at home with beer and Seconal, he was back at his writer's desk.

Superimposed on Faulkner's pattern of daily social drinking and tying one on, now and then, were long benders called "collapses." They were sometimes predictable. Everyone knew, after a book, he would have a collapse. He would have a distant look and be very quiet. Then he would recite poetry. Then he would disappear. Eventually his friends would find him and get him into a hospital. After a few days of rest and paraldehyde, he would be discharged, the picture of health.

Sometimes drying out took longer, particularly at home. Sometimes the Negro help would leave and Estelle would take Jill and go to stay at her mother's house, but commonly members of the family would rotate at Faulkner's bedside, fixing drinks at whatever intervals he called for them. Sometimes he called for a particularly trusted servant, who would find him in a big double bed which he called "Mr. Bill's drunk bed." Faulkner knew that he would not put raw eggs in the drinks, as Estelle might, or Tabasco, as others might. As recalled in the Blotner biography, the servant also had the "gift of conversation to hold him off a little longer, slowly laying the groundwork to bring pappy around. . . ." After he had been on duty for a time he would tell the family, "Mr. Bill ain't never leave off soon from one of these go-rounds. He's restin' a little better now." Blotner said that Faulkner would calculate when he wanted—or needed—to emerge from one of these bouts. After he did, Jill would observe that he would be very quiet for a few days. Then he would say to her, "Missy, I want to talk to you." And then he would apologize to her.

Starting in his thirties, Faulkner's symptoms of alcoholism increased in frequency and severity. He began having withdrawal seizures and delirium tremens. He sometimes vomited blood. He had accidents while drinking, once severely burning his back. Rather late in his drinking career he began having day-long blackouts. He sometimes combined alcohol with drugs, such as Miltown. There is no record though that he abused any substance except alcohol (and of course nicotine). He disliked other alcoholics, calling them disgusting, and was intolerant of his wife's drinking. Personally, he said he liked to drink and never intended to stop. He did stop once for a year in his midthirties, while writing one of his best books, *Light in August*, but it happened only once. He drank, he said, because he liked to drink, because it made him feel good, and taller and stronger, and he liked the taste. He accepted the bruises and fractured vertebrae and other injuries from drinking with stoicism. The symptom he disliked most apparently was the hiccups, which he sometimes had for days after sobering up.

Like Fitzgerald and many other drinkers, Faulkner underwent a marked personality change when he drank, changing from a quiet, reserved, shy man to an exhibitionist. While drinking he would do such things as offer a drink to a passing policeman. The bottle, for Faulkner, was almost a trademark. He posed for MGM publicity stills with a drink in hand. He often wrote with a glass or bottle by his typewriter.

This was not unusual behavior for heavy-drinking celebrities in the thirties. Fats Waller used to play his wonderful stride piano with a bottle of whiskey at his side and never seemed to slur a word or miss a note. The effect of Faulkner's drinking on his writing, however, appears to have been significant. Some critics believed—Hemingway was one—that it explained some of the incoherence. With the stories which really go nowhere and have a thousand loose ends, lacking plot and structure, alcohol may have been the cause. Fitzgerald once said he could never write a novel while drinking because he couldn't keep the plot and characters straight. Faulkner seemed not to worry about it. Once, a cousin asked him, "Do you think up your material when you are drunk?" "Yes, I get a lot of it when I'm drunk," he said. The role of alcohol as muse will be discussed in chapter nine.

One symptom of alcoholism Faulkner, miraculously, never had: cirrhosis. When he died a few hours after a drinking bout, his liver was apparently normal.

Everyone agreed that Faulkner was an alcoholic. That was his diagnosis on his countless hospital admissions. Of all the famous American writers who were alcoholic, Faulkner is widely considered the most severe. His alcoholism had a curious pattern. For long periods he was a normal controlled drinker. Blotner writes: "He'd go along for weeks or months at a normal gait and then the craving would come. Most often he would fight it off but once in a while something would happen that would 'get me all in a turmoil inside,' and liquor seemed the only escape. You would be aware of the increased tension—drumming fingers, evasive looks, monosyllabic replies to questions—then he'd disappear. . . ."

Sometimes Faulkner would plan when to start and plan when to stop, and would not stop until then. His brother John thought he sometimes faked drunkenness—particularly when he wanted to be waited on. Sometimes, according to Blotner, when he was well into a real bout, he would continue to exhibit all the effects even if a friend who was caring for him surreptitiously substituted tea for whiskey. Most of the time, however, there was nothing phony about his drinking. He had a prodigious capacity and drank to oblivion on many, many occasions.

What is curious about Faulkner's pattern is that alcoholics are not *supposed* to be able to combine controlled drinking with binges. A dictum of Alcoholics Anonymous is "all or nothing," meaning that alcoholics have no choice but total abstinence or total intoxication. ("One drink is a drunk.") This raises the possibility that Faulkner had something wrong with him other than alcoholism, or an unusual type of alcoholism.

The famous German psychiatrist Emil Kraepelin described a form of alcoholism called dipsomania, characterized by periodic binges interspersed with long periods of abstinence or moderate drinking. He compared it to manic-depressive disease, an episodic illness in which a person becomes sporadically ill with long periods of normality in between. He speculated that perhaps dipsomaniacs were really manic-depressives who drank when they became depressed or manic.

Both alcoholism and manic-depressive illness run in families. Faulkner had an exceedingly strong history of alcoholism in his family, afflicting at least five known male relatives. There is no known history of manic-depressive disease in the family, but the diagnosis was made not much before the twentieth century. Apparently some psychiatrist gave Faulkner a short course in electroconvulsive therapy (ECT), but the reasons are not known. He had forlorn feelings (like everyone) and occasional feelings of impending doom. He also suffered from insomnia, but the heavy drinking could account for that. He also had claustrophobia and later developed an airplane phobia. This is about the extent of his known psychiatric history. He had a low opinion of people who committed suicide. His wife had tried it once and he was slow to forgive her. When Hemingway committed suicide, Faulkner was critical: "I don't like a man who takes the short way home." He often said he preferred grief to "nothing."

His alcoholism, on the other hand, could be viewed as *slow* suicide (a term used by Karl Menninger). S. Bernard Wortis, his psychiatrist for a short time, said in a letter that Faulkner had "such an intense, emotional responsiveness, such receptiveness for others and their problems, that life was very painful for him. Obviously, his alcoholism was a narcotizing device to make it almost bearable for him. . . . He was a man built to suffer . . . to be unhappy and to make his contribution partly because of this." (Quoted in the Blotner biography, page 568.) There is no question that his drinking was self-destructive and, again, the marvel is that it didn't destroy him until he reached a rather respectable old age.

To conclude this exercise in armchair diagnosis: perhaps Faulkner inherited a "gene" for dipsomania which accounted for the "collapses" and drank the rest of the time—whether normally or in excess—to be sociable or escape everyday tensions (greatly magnified, everyone agrees, in writers and geniuses generally).

Did Faulkner's writing suffer because of his drinking? Was he a better writer because he drank?

The majority opinion is that drinking did more harm than good. There is the general suspicion, for example, that some of his murky writing is that way because he was drunk at time of writing. However, *Light in August,* written when cold sober, is also pretty murky in places, although one of his finest books.

Donald Newlove, a writer who wrote a book about his own drinking *(Those Drinking Days),* thought that alcohol had destroyed Faulkner's talent. "Something disastrous happened when Faulkner turned 49; whatever grip he had on his alcohol faded, and so did the hot focus of his imagination. . . . His brain was stunned by alcohol. What we get is the famous mannered diction, senatorial tone, a hallucinated rhetoric of alcohol full of ravishing if empty glory. Dead junk compared to the sunburst pages of *The Sound and Fury* [believed to be his finest novel, written in his early thirties]."

One can accept Newlove's view only if Faulkner's work in his last sixteen years was junk. Critics disagree about this. His novels always received mixed criticism, ranging from ecstatic to contemptuous. His last book, *The Reivers,* received approximately the same ratio of good-to-bad reviews as his first book, *Soldiers' Pay.* He spent the last eight or ten years of his life writing and rewriting *A Fable* and considered it his magnum opus. It was panned by many American critics, but a Swedish critic compared it to *War and Peace;* again, there is the split between American and European critics, with the latter applauding almost everything Faulkner wrote.

Faulkner himself, in his fifties and sixties, worried that perhaps he was "slowing down," but on the other hand expressed confidence that his current work would equal or surpass anything he had written before. One does *not* see the dramatic decline in quality that one sees in some of his heavy drinking contemporaries—Hemingway, for example.

In truth, Faulkner's brain may have been "stunned" by alcohol but alcohol also may have fueled his genius and given this shy, introspective man the confidence he needed to write. This of course remains speculative, but, for reasons discussed in chapter nine, one cannot dismiss entirely the possibility that alcohol is a source of inspiration for some writers.

Richard Rovere, in an article about Faulkner, divided writers into those who make us privy to human experience and those who *subject* us to it. Faulkner, he believed, belonged to the second group:

> With a writer like Faulkner, when we respond to him at all, we do not so much observe experience as undergo it. We do not recognize a mood; we are overcome by it. . . . It is often impossible to feel *for* Faulkner's characters, but it is almost always possible to feel *with* them. . . . With Faulkner, we come about as close to the simulation of other sensations as it is possible to come in literature, which is to say a good deal closer than, as a rule, it is possible to come in life.

At the same time, Faulkner's characters seem fragmented, divided against themselves. His saving grace was his superlative gifts as a teller of stories. No other serious American writer can match him in the old art of catching the ear of the passerby.

If Faulkner's characters were fragmented, they were no more so than their creator. Faulkner was a consummate role player. His personae included the bohemian artist, the RAF pilot, the country gentleman, the farmer, the fox hunter. As Robert Coughlan has pointed out, the quality that is called creativeness in a writer is closely akin to lying and, in turn, to what undoubtedly Faulkner equated with it, personal honesty. In his capacity to put himself in other persons' skins he was very much like Georges Simenon, and both have been frequently compared to Balzac, thought by many to have been the most gifted novelist who ever lived. Reading Faulkner and Simenon, as Rovere said, we are more overcome by a mood than able to recognize it. Both writers put themselves into a veritable trance when they wrote. Neither would tolerate interruptions. While writing, they *lived* their characters' lives, and perhaps this might partly explain why Faulkner also adopted another role—that of the alcoholic.

Ralph Maloney, a gifted short story writer who died at forty from alcoholism, said that alcoholism, "like accountancy or medicine, is only somebody to be, as are the priesthood, the military and the law . . . So, in the pretty girl's sweet, deliberate wink that we're here, let us be somebody we like. Work for pleasure. Marry a friend."

Faulkner worked for pleasure and married a friend (although they didn't stay friends for long). He would have liked Maloney's credo. Certainly, alcoholism for Faulkner was "somebody to be." He was sometimes accused of faking drunkenness to get attention, playing the role of the drunk (as Fitzgerald did as a child). One then asks, why would he pick this particular role? Why did he drink when drinking was so utterly destructive?

One can suggest three possible reasons: (a) tradition, (b) genes, and (c) the extraordinary tension of role playing, in moving from character to character.

First there was the drinking tradition into which Faulkner was born and which he never questioned and never seemed to want to escape. Corn whiskey was as much a part of turn-of-the-century southern small-town life as were the spinning of yarns and whittling on the courthouse lawn. It was something exclusive for men. There was always whiskey on the hunting trips to be consumed around the fireside in a spirit of masculine camaraderie, perhaps only seen elsewhere in wartime. Drinking, for Faulkner, was associated with honor, chivalry, achievement. His great-grandfather and grandfather drank inordinately and Faulkner admired them both and wanted to be like them. Storytelling and drinking were often inseparable. There was no guilt attached to drinking and little to drunkenness. His grandfather once got drunk and threw a brick through his bank window, explaining that he had every right to do so since it was his brick and his bank. Drinking and violence were all mixed together, as they were in Faulkner's stories. Drinking and a world without women: both appealed to Faulkner immensely. He had a low opinion of women (at least women in the abstract). He thought they were different from men. He once said that women were impervious to evil, meaning women were born psychopaths who couldn't be trusted. He thought marriages were bad, all marriages, but stayed married to one woman because he didn't see any point in changing. He thought Hemingway was a fool to keep changing wives, since marriages and wives were all the same. He had a series of young mistresses but was never a libertine. On the contrary, he was somewhat prudish, disliking pornography (although many of his books were considered pornographic). Drinking was something one did with men, part of its attraction for Faulkner. Finally, the alcohol those southern men drank was strong alcohol. Wine and beer were considered distinctly inferior to products of the local still or a good brand of bourbon, if one could afford it. Getting drunk may not always have been the drinker's intention, but getting drunk was awfully easy with white corn whiskey.

So, growing up in a small southern town in the early twentieth century, in a distinguished family of heavy drinkers who went off and got "cured" for their alcoholism as casually as they would have a wart removed, produced in Faulkner a feeling that drinking was a normal activity, with risk attached, but risk worth taking. Brother Jack said that if William had had a choice between living a short life with liquor and living a long life without it, he certainly would have chosen the former. As it turned out, he had both: liquor and a rather long life.

Then there was the bohemian tradition which Faulkner, in his formative years, discovered in Greenwich Village, the French Quarter in New Orleans, and, for a time, the Left Bank of Paris. Heavy drinking was part of life in these places. It was part of being a writer—a genius. "All good writers are drunkards," Hemingway told Fitzgerald. Drinking was expected of writers. Drunkenness was expected. As long as the writers of the twenties could produce "great" art from time to time, drinking was not only tolerated but encouraged, at least covertly. The gifted alcoholic writer became a cult figure, a model for less gifted writers to follow into the later part of the century.

Now, concerning genes: alcoholism runs in families and it certainly ran in Faulkner's. There is evidence that a tendency to alcoholism is inherited. Whether Faulkner's alcoholism was inherited or, like his southern accent, a product of his circumstances will never be known, but the *extent* of the alcoholism among the Faulkner males would suggest a force more powerful than "role modeling."

Finally, Faulkner was not one man but many. His inconsistencies, Coughlan noted in 1953, went beyond artistic license or mere eccentricity. "His is not a split personality but rather a fragmented one, loosely held together by some strong inner force, the pieces often askew and sometimes painfully in friction." Coughlan attributed the drinking to the friction. "It is to ease these pains, one can guess, that he escapes periodically and sometimes for periods of weeks in alcoholism, until his drinking has become legendary in his profession." Coughlan then made a rather curious observation—that William Faulkner was not an alcoholic but an "alcoholic refugee, self-pursued."

If William Faulkner was not an alcoholic, then the concept of alcoholism should be abandoned once and for all.

Coughlan, in fact, contradicts himself later:

> The taciturnity, the contemplation, the appearance of aloof and unheeding purposefulness disguised a conflict whose nature was confided to no one but was of such intensity that he was driven to escape. His alcoholic holidays from reality as he saw it became a necessary fixture of his life . . . but generally they were as unobtrusive as his normal behavior. He would supply himself with whiskey and, after a period of elation, retire to his own bed, drinking until sleep or coma set in, drinking again when consciousness returned, until days and nights had passed and slowly he returned to the world. At such times his friends and relatives would come and sit with him, taking turns so that he always had attention and care, as with a man suffering any other serious illness.

That is not alcoholism?

Elsewhere in this book, it is suggested that alcoholism is a "disease of individualism." Faulkner was an individualist par excellence. Quoting Coughlan again.:

> Life had no meaning, in Faulkner's writing, except to the individual. There is no moral code beyond what in an older day might have been called the "code of the gentleman": courage and honor

and pride and pity and love of justice and liberty. But to keep this code brings no rewards beyond self-respect, it brings no salvation, no protection, for the "good" and "bad" characters are damned impartially to futility.

Coughlan concludes his Faulkner piece rhapsodically:

. . . All the immense cast of characters Faulkner has assembled and the robbery, incest, murder, suicide, fratricide, dope addiction, alcoholism, idiocy, insanity, grave robbery, miscegenation, necrophilia, adultery, fornication, prostitution, lynching, selfishness, ingratitude, whoring, gallantry and courage which embellishes plots are not the recordings of a naturalist but the symbolic expressions of Faulkner's outrage and revulsion about what he conceived to be the tragedy of William Faulkner, of his age and of the man.

One last question needs asking: What kind of writer would Faulkner have been if he hadn't been alcoholic? Would he have been a writer at all? The questions are unanswerable. In Faulkner's case— more than appears to be true of the other writers in this book— writing and drinking were so intertwined that one is justified in thinking that one could not have existed without the other. Faulkner *had* to relax; alcohol did it for him. He had to fantasize; alcohol did this for him. He had to shift from world to world, from character to character, from persona to persona, with as little friction as possible, and alcohol did this for him.

There are other good writers who drink little or not at all. The chances are that Faulkner would not have been one of them.

Still, what do we really know? What we really know is that, over a fifty-year span, while decimating acres of corn, Faulkner wrote nineteen novels, scores of short stories, hundreds of poems, and dozens of screenplays. He won the Nobel Prize, the Pulitzer Prize, and the Legion of Honor. Edmund Wilson called him a genius. Hemingway called him America's greatest writer (Hemingway called *no one* a genius). Camus called him the *world's* greatest writer. *Time* compared him to Shakespeare. Even some of his neighbors in Oxford, Mississippi, thought he was pretty good—if you liked dirty books.

Bibliographical Note

Faulkner scholars and admirers are fortunate to have a two-volume, almost day-by-day account of Faulkner's life which is also warmly and sometimes beautifully written. This is Joseph Blotner's *Faulkner: A Biography* (New York: Random House, 1974). The work was reissued in 1984 in one volume, much revised. A scholar and English professor, Blotner was a personal friend of Faulkner's. Although semiofficial, the biography includes warts and all. The Blotner biography was an invaluable source for this chapter.

Faulkner's brother John was also a professional writer (*Men Working; Dollar Cotton*) and died soon after William's death. Perhaps his best work was *My Brother Bill: An Affectionate Reminiscence* (New York: Trident Press, 1963). Another brother, Murry (Jack), was an FBI agent and not a professional writer, but *his* book about William, *The Falkners of Mississippi: A Memoir* (Baton Rouge: Louisiana State University Press, 1967), displays the Faulkner literary genes on every page (and also explains why some Faulkners have the *u* in their name and others don't).

A small biographical classic resulted from visits by Robert Coughlan to Oxford in the early 1950s, leading to a two-part series on Faulkner in *Life* magazine. It was published as a book, *The Private World of William Faulkner* (New York: Harper and Brothers, 1954), now out of print. It is worth going to the library to dig out the *Life* articles, which appeared on 28 September and 5 October 1953. Coughlan's descriptions of Faulkner the man, the real world he lived in, and the imaginary one he created, are incomparable (and the pictures alone justify the library visit).

Other sources for this chapter were *The Faulkner–Cowley File: Letters and Memories, 1944–1962* by Malcolm Cowley (New York: Viking Press, 1966); *Count No'Count: Flashbacks to Faulkner* by Ben Wasson (Jackson: University Press of Mississippi, 1983); *William Faulkner of Oxford*, edited by James W. Webb and A. Wigfall Green (Baton Rouge: Louisiana State University Press, 1965); *Faulkner: A Comprehensive Guide to the Brodsky Collection*, vols. 1 and 2, edited by Louis Daniel Brodsky and Robert W. Hamblin (Jackson: University Press of Mississippi, 1983–84); *Faulkner: The Transfiguration of Biography* by Judith B. Wittenberg (Lincoln: University of Nebraska Press, 1979).

7

O'NEILL
Alcohol and the Irish

*Altogether too much damned nonsense has been written about
the dissipation of artists.*

O'Neill

Two psychiatrists have won the Nobel Prize in medicine—Julius
Wagner-Jauregg for the malarial treatment of neurosyphilis, and
Antonio Moniz for promoting lobotomy. More deserving than
either, perhaps, was Gilbert V. Hamilton. As a young New York
psychoanalyst in the mid-1920s, Hamilton converted America's
greatest playwright from a ferocious alcoholic into a dedicated teetotaler, and did it all in six weeks.

In the process he may also have transformed his patient, Eugene
O'Neill, from a spectacularly productive playwright into a recluse
who went twelve years without having a play on Broadway, but this
cannot be proved. His cure of O'Neill's drinking problem, on the
other hand, surely must represent one of the outstanding medical
triumphs of the century.

It all happened in a most peculiar manner.

Hamilton had received a grant to survey the sexual practices of
married people. His subjects included Mr. and Mrs. Eugene
O'Neill. Hamilton later received funds for a six-week "psychoanalysis" of six subjects. O'Neill agreed to be one of them. After six
weeks O'Neill decided he loved and hated his father and had an
Oedipus complex. Hamilton decided O'Neill had a death wish.
Whatever the explanation, O'Neill, at thirty-seven, stopped drinking. Except for two or three lapses—only one of them serious—he
stayed sober until his death twenty-eight years later.

Hamilton's achievement was remarkable for several reasons.

One is that psychiatrists are generally skeptical about their ability to help alcoholics; some refuse even to try. Also, O'Neill's therapy was brief; even those psychiatrists who consider alcoholism treatable usually expect the treatment to last practically forever. Finally, O'Neill had a malignant form of the disease. He was a "gamma" alcoholic, E.M. Jellinek's term for the alcoholic incapable of drinking at all without drinking to the bitter end. He was Irish; he came from a drinking family; his friends and wife drank; he had suicidal depressions; and he wrote. Not only did he write, he was a famous writer, and famous American writers in the 1920s were more often alcoholic than not.

To understand why O'Neill stopped drinking it is necessary to examine how he began. From his own work (he was probably the most autobiographical playwright in history) and the voluminous writings about him, it is possible to do this, combining as little "damned nonsense" with as much historical fact as the record will allow.

O'Neill was born in 1888 in a New York City hotel, the son of a famous Irish-American actor. During his early childhood Eugene traveled with his parents from city to city where his father, a matinee idol of the period, starred as the count in *The Count of Monte Cristo,* a role he played for twenty-nine years. His father hated the role, his mother hated travel, and Eugene hated hotels. His last words, uttered before his death in a Boston hotel, were, "Born in a damned hotel, died in a damned hotel." The family owned a house in New London, Connecticut, where they spent the summers, and this was closest to a permanent home that Eugene ever was to know.

O'Neill spent his boyhood and adolescence in boarding schools, feeling lonely and abandoned. Summers in New London were his happiest times. He was particularly close to his older brother Jamie, whom he idolized, emulated, and finally immortalized in two almost purely autobiographical plays, *Long Day's Journey into Night* and *A Moon for the Misbegotten.*

At eighteen O'Neill attended Princeton for a year. Flunking out, he worked for a time as a secretary in New York. At twenty he married on impulse, then fled to Honduras to prospect for gold. His first son, Eugene O'Neill, Jr., was born during his absence. O'Neill never lived with his first wife. She eventually divorced him. He first met his son when the boy was twelve.

O'Neill's life from his Princeton days until age twenty-five was aimless and chaotic. Part of the time was spent at sea. He sailed to Buenos Aires on a windjammer and became a waterfront bum. Working his way home as a sailor, he later became a seaman on a luxury liner, traveling to Southampton and back. Between voyages he lived in a flophouse saloon near the New York waterfront, sustained by a small allowance from his father. Following a suicide attempt at twenty-three, he traveled for a time with his father, playing bit parts in his father's perennial potboiler. Unhappy as ever, he finally got a job as a cub reporter for a New London newspaper, where he obtained the reputation (deserved or not) of being the worst reporter in the paper's history.

During these years—his late adolescence and early twenties—O'Neill read, drank, whored, despaired, wrote poetry, and collected, unknowingly, a stockpile of experiences that would fuel his plays for years to come. He lacked the faintest notion of what he wanted to do except, vaguely, "write," especially write poetry. His poetry was never very good and he realized it; even this goal was a source of despair.

Through his life O'Neill had many illnesses: rickets as a child, malaria when in Honduras, tuberculosis during his twenties, and finally the illness that killed him, the insidious, mysterious neurological affliction that began in adolescence with a tremor and left him a helpless cripple during the last years of his life. Of these, only tuberculosis had a redeeming feature, for it was during five months in a sanatorium, at twenty-five, that O'Neill decided to be a playwright. Having made the decision, he produced plays at a ferocious pace: good plays, bad plays, terrible plays, and two or three great plays, as great as any produced in modern times.

Within two years O'Neill turned out an astounding quantity of work, including eleven one-act plays, three full-length plays, a number of unproduced film scenarios, poems, and several short stories. His first one-act play was produced at twenty-eight, his first full-length play, *Beyond the Horizon*, four years later. By then, O'Neill was considered America's most promising (and certainly most prolific) playwright. For the next fourteen years at least one O'Neill play appeared in a New York theater each year, often two or three simultaneously.

During these years O'Neill was married again; had two children by his second wife; was divorced and remarried; made large amounts of money; spent most of it; hobnobbed with literary friends; became world-famous; lived for a time, it seems, almost everywhere—Cape Cod, New York, Connecticut, Long Island, Georgia, Bermuda, Europe—buying expensive houses and selling them; and all the while writing and drinking, drinking and writing (at least until his psychoanalysis, when writing and drinking were replaced by writing and wanting to drink).

O'Neill continued writing year after year until, late in life, his tremor made the physical act impossible (he never mastered dictation). But in his midforties a curious thing happened: his plays stopped being produced. From 1934 to 1946 not one new O'Neill play opened. The apparent reason is even more curious. It was not that O'Neill's talent dried up or his plays were less in demand. The reason was not that he no longer wrote. It was that he could no longer *stop* writing.

In writing, sculpture, and other arts, the trick is not so much what is put in as what is left out. O'Neill was never a good leaver-outer. His critics complained that his plays were overlong and repetitious; so did his producers, actors, and audiences. Ignoring them, O'Neill kept writing longer and longer plays, the *reductio ad absurdum* being *Mourning Becomes Electra*, a thirteen-act marathon that began at five and lasted until midnight.

Mourning was one of O'Neill's last plays before his work stopped appearing on Broadway. It was part of O'Neill's most grandiose project: a cycle of plays reconstructing the entirety of American history, from colonial times to the present. The longer O'Neill worked on the cycle, the longer and more numerous the plays became (he first planned five, then seven, then eleven). And, after *Mourning*, he decided that none should be produced until all were completed. All were never completed, and one of the most poignant scenes of O'Neill's life is of the dying playwright and his wife sitting before a fireplace and destroying the finished plays, one by one. (One play,

A Touch of the Poet, survived and was produced after O'Neill's death.)

Fortunately for theatergoers, on three occasions O'Neill put aside his cycle to produce two masterpieces. In 1940, at fifty-two, he wrote probably his finest play, *Long Day's Journey into Night,* a harrowing account of the stormy O'Neill family during a New London summer in 1912. He also wrote *The Iceman Cometh.* The last new play produced during his lifetime, *Iceman* appeared in 1946. His third noncycle play, *A Moon for the Misbegotten,* artistically inferior to the two others, is a moving account of his brother Jamie's capitulation to drink and despair.

Meanwhile, O'Neill and his third wife continued their restless search for the perfect home. They lived for a time near Seattle, then settled down for the war years in a house near San Francisco, then returned East to live in and around New York and Boston. Wherever they lived, it was almost always in seclusion. When O'Neill stopped drinking, he also stopped—except for brief interludes—socializing.

O'Neill had an Irishman's superstition about cursed families, his own included. The last years of his life did little to dispel the belief. His favorite child, Eugene, Jr., a distinguished classical scholar at Yale, became alcoholic and committed suicide. His other son, Shane, was a narcotics addict. At eighteen his beautiful daughter, Oona, married Charlie Chaplin—a man the same age as O'Neill— and O'Neill never forgave her, refusing to have her name mentioned in his presence for the rest of his life.

Then there was his illness. His famous minuscule handwriting (he once wrote a three-act play on two and a half pages) became progressively unreadable. In his last years he could not write at all— surely the most agonizing deprivation fate could devise for a man as addicted to writing as his sons were to alcohol and heroin. His legs became affected and he had trouble walking. He was hospitalized for long periods—once for chronic bromide intoxication. Finally, at sixty-five, after years of wanting to die and being unable to do so, he succumbed to pneumonia in a Boston hotel.

His illness had been diagnosed as Parkinson's disease, but autopsy revealed a rare cerebellar degenerative disorder, perhaps familial, since O'Neill's mother also had a tremor.

This, then, was O'Neill's life—as tragic as any tragedy he ever wrote—and this was the background against which his drinking began and ended.

It began in infancy. Whenever baby Eugene had a nightmare or stomachache, his father gave him a few drops of whiskey in water. O'Neill later believed this old Irish custom contributed to his drinking problem.

His nonmedicinal use of alcohol began at fifteen, and began, he indicated later, not casually but in earnest. During summer vacations he drank with his brother in New London bars. By the time O'Neill was eighteen his brother also introduced him to New London brothels—Eugene's first experience with sex—and both were getting intoxicated regularly.

His alcohol consumption increased during his Princeton year, when he developed a taste for absinthe, a wormwood-alcohol combination now outlawed in most countries because of its toxicity (see chapter one). Classmates of O'Neill, interviewed by biographer Louis Sheaffer, recalled that he "used to wander off into the most fantastic and exotic excursions of the mind" while drinking absinthe, and often came home in a condition of "extreme and sometimes crazy intoxication." One time his bar buddies, instead of bringing him home, carried him to the cemetery and left him on Aaron Burr's grave. His Princeton friends looked upon him as a wild Irishman. "For all his usual reserve, he would be explosively articulate when liquored up. His thick black hair tumbling over his forehead, heavy eyebrows adding exclamation marks to his flashing eyes, arms waving freely, his face flushed, he would hold forth—atop a chair or table—about everything." Once, "berserk with absinthe," he smashed up furniture in a dormitory room, and found a revolver and pulled the trigger several times, but the gun was empty. His friends tied him up with bed sheets and he passed out. Suspended from Princeton after a drunken prank, O'Neill later flunked out because of poor grades—poor, at least partly, because of alcohol and wormwood.

By his late teens there was no doubt about O'Neill's drinking problem. No doubt, perhaps, except in O'Neill's mind. From his viewpoint, he was simply following the example of his father and brother. His father drank daily, usually in barrooms, but boasted that he never missed a performance because of liquor. "You brought him up to be a boozer," says Eugene's mother to his father in *Long Day's Journey into Night*. "Since he first opened his eyes, he's seen you drinking. Always a bottle on the bureau in the cheap hotel rooms." However, Eugene's habits were modeled more after his brother's. Jamie practically lived in bars and brothels and went on titanic binges. So, during his early twenties, did Eugene, but with a difference. Jamie preferred classy bars and extravagant living; Eugene found his niche in the lower depths of society, on Buenos Aires' waterfront and New York's Lower West Side. He lived with bums, drank with bums, and ultimately wrote about bums.

From the beginning O'Neill's drinking was periodic in nature. When he drank, he usually got drunk, and as he got older, the drunks carried over into the next day and became binges. But when the binge ended—because he was too sick or too broke to drink any longer—O'Neill suffered through the hangover and went to work. Before writing plays, work consisted of reading omnivorously and writing poetry. Until his "cure" at thirty-seven, O'Neill's life was devoted almost exclusively to drinking or work. He did not mix them. "You've got to have all your critical and creative faculties about you when you're working," O'Neill said. "I never try to write a line when I'm not strictly on the wagon."

O'Neill was always fascinated with "rhythm," referring often to the "rhythm of life" and the rhythm in his plays. His own life was dominated by rhythm—the systole of creative work, the diastole of drink—until Dr. Hamilton eliminated the diastole.

Success, unlike Dr. Hamilton, did little to relieve O'Neill's drinking problem. Soon after becoming affluent he went on a $100 drunk, fulfilling a long-time ambition. Nor did Prohibition help. During his down-and-out days O'Neill had made many friends among gangsters who later kept him well supplied with bootleg whiskey. In Jamie's case the death of a parent helped; when his father died he went on the wagon and stayed there until his mother's death two years later. Not so with Eugene; he got drunk after each parent's death, as well as Jamie's.

As an adult, O'Neill usually was a quiet drunk, but not always. On several occasions he assaulted his wife Agnes. She described "dreadful outbursts of violence . . . when he appeared more like a madman than anything else." One college friend noted that O'Neill did not need to drink heavily to "reach a state of ferocity." He had "too much motor for the chassis," the friend explained. "When the mood was on him, you could sense the potentialities in the man for destruction and trouble."

It is unclear when O'Neill first acknowledged his alcoholism. He had monumental hangovers, but his regimen for treating them ("taper off slowly with carefully timed drinks and judicious infusions of soup and milk shakes, interspersed with periods of sleep and exercise") apparently was effective; he never experienced frank delirium tremens. He made a strenuous effort to pace himself during binges. One ploy was to open the *Saturday Evening Post* and read whatever he came across, alternating stories with drinks. O'Neill's friends also tried to help, locking him in bedrooms and basements, but other friends surreptitiously supplied him with liquor.

When O'Neill was thirty-five, at the height of his fame, his brother Jamie died of alcoholism. This, as well as Dr. Hamilton's treatment, may have helped him achieve sobriety two years later. Eugene was often with Jamie in his final days, sharing a bottle as they had done for years. Eugene's drinking was never heavier. "Not infrequently," biographers Arthur and Barbara Gelb report, "both brothers were ill enough to require medical treatment."

When his brother died, Eugene made heroic attempts to go on the wagon, since he was convinced drinking would kill him as it had his brother. Finally he yielded to his friends' urgings and sought psychiatric help. His first psychiatrist was Smith Ely Jellife, whom O'Neill chose because he was not a psychoanalyst. Like many writers of the time, O'Neill, although fascinated with Freudian theory, feared that a personal psychoanalysis would ruin his talent. He saw Dr. Jellife for two years to "talk things over." Except for six months in Bermuda, when he limited his drinking to a glass of ale before supper, he continued to drink heavily.

Then came Dr. Hamilton's sex survey and O'Neill's six-week psychoanalysis. Thereafter he banned alcohol from his home, shunned his drinking friends, and with his beautiful third wife, an actress, went into seclusion lasting most of the rest of his life. He fell off the wagon three times—the longest episode was in Shanghai and ended in a medical ward—but otherwise, except for a rare sip of beer or champagne in his later years, O'Neill never again drank alcohol.

Inevitably, the urge to speculate about why O'Neill drank and why he stopped—the "damned nonsense" he complained about—becomes irresistible. O'Neill himself indulged in such speculation; so did his friends and biographers. The theories generally run along these lines:

First, there was heredity. O'Neill's maternal grandfather, an Irish immigrant, became an alcoholic in his forties. O'Neill's paternal grandfather also immigrated to America from Ireland, then abandoned the family, returned to Ireland, and may have committed suicide (O'Neill only hints at the possibility). O'Neill's father was a heavy drinker. O'Neill's mother for twenty-five years was a morphine addict and once attempted suicide. O'Neill's brother died of alcoholism. O'Neill's two sons were, respectively, an alcoholic and an opiate addict.

Alcoholism runs in families. No one knows whether heredity plays a role. O'Neill's alcoholism may have originated in his genes but this cannot be proved; there was also his environment—nature and nurture are usually inseparable.

"I'm all Irish," O'Neill said, referring not only to his ancestry but also to the Irish customs and attitudes of his family, exquisitely portrayed in *Long Day's Journey into Night*. In the play, as John Henry Raleigh has pointed out, a bottle of whiskey is at the center of the room, in many ways its most important object. "If not using it, they talk about it. It enters into their very characters; the father's penuriousness is most neatly summed up by the fact that he keeps his liquor under lock and key and has an eagle eye for the exact level of the whiskey in the bottle. . . . By the same token, the measure of the sons' rebellion is how much liquor they can 'sneak.'"

Raleigh believes that "sneaking a drink" has more significance for the Irish than any other cultural group. "Allied to this peculiarly Irish custom are the concomitant phrase and action: 'watering the whiskey,' that is, filling the bottle with water to the level where it was before you 'sneaked your drink.'" In some Irish households, Raleigh says, "whole cases of whiskey slowly evolve into a watery, brown liquid, without the bottles having ever been set forth socially, so to speak. This act—the lonely, surreptitious, rapid gulp of whiskey—is the national rite. . . ."

National or not, it was clearly an O'Neill family rite, as was another custom traditionally Irish: the medicinal use of alcohol.

"The Irish addiction to drink is a simplifying element in their lives," writes Raleigh. "This is how all problems are met—to reach for the bottle." And reach the O'Neills did. "A drop now and then is no harm when you're in low spirits, or have a bad cold," advises the maid in *Long Day's Journey*, and Eugene's father agreed. "I've always found good whiskey the best of tonics," he says in the play, calling drink the "good man's failing." Even O'Neill's mother found alcohol a "healthy stimulant."

According to Irish scholars, alcohol served utilitarian functions other than medicinal, at least in earlier times. The Irish were as Puritanical about sex as they were tolerant toward drunkenness, and in fact the two were linked: alcohol served as a sexual substitute. The teetotaler, indeed, was considered a menace, a man who prowled the streets getting girls into trouble. When a young man was unhappy in love, he was advised to "drink it off." According to Arensberg and Kimball, "Drowning one's sorrows becomes the expected means of relief, much as prayer among women." Unhappiness in love was often the occasion for O'Neill's binges.

As noted above, when O'Neill stopped drinking he also stopped socializing, also Irish-like. In Ireland, according to M.J.F. McCarthy, it is a "deadly insult to refuse to take a drink from a man, unless an elaborate explanation and apology be given and accepted." As Arensberg and Kimball put it, "Drinking together is the traditional reaffirmation of solidarity and equality among males." O'Neill was incapable of elaborate apology; rather than try, he gave up male companionship.

O'Neill's family and wives (until the third) were exceptionally tolerant of his drinking—another Irish trait. Among the Irish, Arensberg and Kimball say, drunkenness is "laughable, pleasurable, a punctuation of dull routine to be watched and applauded, and drunken men are handled with care and affection." Even mothers refer to a drunken son as the "the poor boy," with "sympathy, love, pity, and sorrow."

O'Neill's mother, who had her own problem with morphine, may not have responded in quite this manner, but his second wife, who lived with his drunkenness for years, apparently did. She once confided to a friend that she had fallen in love with O'Neill and married him because he was drunk all the time and needed her help.

O'Neill's Irish ancestry and upbringing may explain his choice of palliatives, alcohol, but not his need for palliation. The need had ample sources.

First, there was guilt about his mother. Her morphinism began with his birth. He weighed eleven pounds; the delivery was so difficult her physician gave her morphine, to which she became addicted for the next twenty-five years. O'Neill learned about her addiction at fifteen, the year he began drinking. Until then he had been either puzzled or frightened by her behavior. "She used to drift around the house like a ghost," he later wrote about their New London years. "I didn't know what was wrong and kept trying to reach her." Now that he knew about his mother's addiction, he also knew its cause—his birth. The knowledge produced a guilt she did little to assuage.

About this time he also abandoned his Roman Catholic faith. God, as it were, became as unreachable as his mother. She had wanted him to be a priest. The occasions for guilt multiplied.

O'Neill's need for palliation also arose from social insecurity and a shyness and sensitivity stemming from early childhood. Whether traveling with his parents or attending boarding school or summering in New London, he felt he never "belonged"—one of his favorite words—and he hoarded grievances concerning his real and imagined rejection. His literary ambition, as he later wrote, was fired to some extent by the "small-boy ambition . . . to chortle triumphantly: 'Look, Teacher! See what I have done!' "—to gain, in short, the acceptance denied him in childhood.

Drinking served the same function as writing; he *felt* accepted when drunk, and his shyness left him. Sober, he was taciturn and reserved; drunk, he became gregarious and verbose. George Jean Nathan once speculated that if O'Neill "hadn't drunk the way he did and mixed with many kinds of people in those early days, we probably shouldn't have had his plays." When George Bernard Shaw, a lifelong teetotaler, heard that O'Neill had quit drinking, he predicted O'Neill would never again write a good play. He was almost right.

O'Neill was preoccupied with insanity—the subject dominates a half dozen of his plays—and it is unclear whether he had a psychiatric illness other than alcoholism. It appears likely. He was "born afraid," in his mother's words, and throughout his life had phobias—for example, of thunderstorms and crowds. "Behind his quiet manner," a friend wrote, "there is a tenseness of nerves, which his long, thin fingers emphasize as they beat a tattoo on his thigh or dig themselves into the palms of his hands."

Always gloomy and pessimistic ("hopeless hope" was a favorite expression), he also had dark and prolonged depressions in the clinical sense. He spoke often of suicide; in his twenties he almost succeeded in killing himself with an overdose of barbiturates (interestingly, he had been sober for a time before making the attempt). In moments of despair he contemplated swimming out into the ocean until drowning. ("But I'm too good a swimmer," he wryly told a friend, "and would probably instinctively save myself.") His plays reveal an "infatuation with oblivion," as Brooks Atkinson put it. He was reckless in ways other than with alcohol; he was a maniacally fast driver, a daredevil swimmer.

Dr. Hamilton's cure of O'Neill's alcoholism did not cure his depressions, which persisted until his death. In his last years, according to biographers Arthur and Barbara Gelb, he dwelt more and more on suicide and "deplored the vestiges of Catholic indoctrination" which held him back.

Heredity, environment, depression—all may have contributed to his alcoholism, but in what proportion and to what extent it is impossible to know. Nor can it be known with certainty why he stopped drinking. By the time he saw Dr. Hamilton he had finally acknowledged his alcoholism. He had been profoundly shaken by his brother's death. And he had become concerned about his health. Recalled a New York doctor who knew him at the time: "He talked a great deal about his health, and one day he asked me to listen to his heart, explaining that it was 'out of place,' located in the middle of his chest."

Finally, there were O'Neill's famous stubbornness and determination to write at all costs. "I'd like to see anyone influence [Eugene] more than he wants to be," says Jamie in *Long Day's Journey*. "His quietness fools people into thinking they can do what they like with him. But he's stubborn as hell inside and what he does is what he wants to do, and to hell with anyone else." What O'Neill wanted to do more than anything—more than drink—was to write plays. "One drink and I'm off," he told his wife, and being off meant more than suffering and death; it meant not writing, an intolerable prospect for O'Neill.

So Dr. Hamilton had these things going for him. What he did with them—how he managed that final twist of the screw that produced enduring sobriety—is not recorded. Perhaps his success surprised him as much as it did O'Neill.

What effect did sobriety have on O'Neill's writing? O'Neill missed alcohol, the way it relaxed him and helped him forget. He felt sobriety left a "void" in his fantasy life and, in a letter, said he missed the "companionable . . . intensely dramatic phantoms and obsessions, which, with caressing claws in my heart and brain, led me for weeks at a time down the ever-changing vistas of that No-Man's-Land between the DT's and the Reality."

William James once called drunkenness "the great Yea-sayer, sobriety the great Nay-sayer." If O'Neill had kept drinking, he might have better controlled his obsessive-criticalness, his inability to say "yea" to a completed work. Without alcohol, there was nothing to interrupt the rhythm of his writing. Once, when dissatisfied with a scene, he wrote, "Maybe, if I were a drinking man, I would have seen it more clearly at the start. There are times in the writing of drama when a bit of cloudiness can bring a sudden gleam of light more effectively than too-long studious analysis." Like all writers, he was at the mercy of the Muse. "Little unconscious mind," he once prayed, "bring home the bacon." Perhaps alcohol helped bring it home.

Recovering from alçoholism, O'Neill wrote, is "like getting over leprosy. One misses playing solitaire with one's scales." Still, alcohol might well have killed him before he wrote two of America's finest plays. In the end his talent survived sobriety.

Bibliographical Note

The account of O'Neill's psychoanalysis is contained in *O'Neill* by Arthur and Barbara Gelb (New York: Harper and Brothers, 1960). This formidable biography examines O'Neill's life and work in minute detail and is immensely readable. Equally valuable is Louis Sheaffer's beautifully written *O'Neill, Son and Playwright* (Boston: Little, Brown & Co., 1968).

As important as his biographers for source materials were O'Neill's highly autobiographical plays. Most are contained in *The Plays of Eugene O'Neill*, 3 vols.(New York: Random House, 1951). Other plays were subsequently published by Random House and Yale University Press. Five unpublished plays are available in the Library of Congress and the Houghton Library at Harvard University.

Other helpful sources were Agnes Boulton's *Part of a Long Story* (Garden City, N.Y.: Doubleday, 1958). Normand Berlin's *Eugene O'Neill* (New York: Grove, 1982), Frederick Carpenter's *Eugene O'Neill*, rev. ed. (New York: G.K. Hall, 1979), Harry C. Cronin's *Eugene O'Neill: Irish and American* (New York: Ayer Co., 1976), Virginia Floyd's *Eugene O'Neill: A World View* (New York: Ungar, 1980), and John Gassner's *O'Neill: A Collection of Critical Essays* (Englewood Cliffs, N.J.: Prentice-Hall, 1964). The last contains a highly imaginative essay by John Henry Raleigh about O'Neill's New England Irish-Catholic background. Other sources consulted about Irish drinking customs were Conrad M. Arensberg and Solon T. Kimball's *The Irish Countryman* (New York: Macmillan Co., 1937),

M.J.F. McCarthy's *Irish Land and Irish Liberty* (London: Robert Scott, 1911), and an excellent review of these and other works by Robert F. Bales, "Attitudes Toward Drinking in the Irish Culture," in *Society, Culture, and Drinking Patterns* (New York: John Wiley & Sons, 1962).

8

LOWRY
Canadian Paradise

*Gin and orange juice are the best cure for alcoholism, the real
cause of which is ugliness and the complete baffling sterility of
existence as sold to you.*

Lowry, "Through the Panama"

For as long as there are serious readers of literature, Malcolm Lowry
will be remembered for one accomplishment: a novel called *Under
the Volcano*. Published in 1947, it was instantly acclaimed a masterpiece. Lowry was ranked with Dante, Melville, and Joyce as a writer for the ages.

It took Lowry ten years to write *Under the Volcano*. When he died
ten years later, at forty-eight, not a single additional word of Lowry's had appeared in print. His lifetime published work consisted of
Under the Volcano and a romantic novel written in his youth called
Ultramarine, plus a few stories and poems.

Lowry's literary output, however, vastly exceeded his published
work. When he died, he left behind thousands of pages of manuscripts consisting of poems, sketches, stories, and novels so rambling and disjointed that publication was inconceivable. Inconceivable or not, thanks to the reputation of *Under the Volcano*, four volumes were salvaged for posthumous publication—a collection of
short stories, two unfinished novels, and a remarkable novella,
twenty years in the writing, called *Lunar Caustic*. This, plus his collected letters, a first-rate biography by Douglas Day, some volumes
of literary criticism, and a continuous stream of Ph.D. theses and
learned articles in little magazines, represents the sum total of what
we know about Lowry's life and writings.

We know one thing more: Lowry was an alcoholic who drank

almost every day of his life, from adolescence to his death, and whose alcoholism permeates his works to an extent unparalleled in literature.

For reasons about which one can only speculate, Lowry was in partial control of his drinking during just one period of his life, the years spent in Canada between 1939 and 1954 (with drunken interludes in New York, Mexico, Paris, and elsewhere). This period of relative sobriety—never more than relative—was when he wrote most of *Under the Volcano*. Lowry, his wife, and friends agreed that Canada deserved at least part of the credit for his control (and, thus, the creation of a masterpiece). Precisely how all those years living in a beach shack on Vancouver Bay kept a gargantuan drinker like Lowry more or less in control will be explored later.

Canada, at any rate, has often claimed Lowry as its own. The Malcolm Lowry collection at the library of the University of British Columbia includes numerous Lowry manuscripts. *Canadian Literature* has published many articles about Lowry as well as compiled bibliographies of his unpublished works. When *Under the Volcano* was dramatized on the radio in 1947, Lowry was eulogized as "Canada's greatest, most successful writer" (although he was born, raised, and educated in England). Lowry missed the broadcast, and the praise; his radio battery was dead. Perhaps it was just as well—the dramatization wasn't good and praise invariably launched Lowry on a bender. In any case, Lowry, the insatiable symbol seeker, probably added dead batteries to his list of demons.

There are two ways to approach Malcolm Lowry: enigma, mystic, genius, alcoholic. One is to see him from the outside, as others saw him. The other is to see him from the inside, to observe his thoughts and feelings. The latter is possible with Lowry to a degree probably impossible with any other writer except Proust. Lowry was incapable of writing about any other subject than himself. His works, published and unpublished, consist almost exclusively of his thoughts and feelings about himself, his work, his alcoholism, and, almost in passing, the world around him.

One way to speculate about how others saw Lowry is to examine, chronologically, his photographs in the biography by Douglas Day.

There are nearly fifty of them. Studying them, one is reminded of a quotation from Jean Cocteau's play *La Machine infernale* (Lowry saw the play several times and it was perhaps the main shaping force of *Under the Volcano*): "Behold, spectator, wound up to the full, so that its spring slowly uncoils throughout the length of human life, one of the most perfect machines built by the Gods of the abyss for the mathematical destruction of a human life."

Just as in the novel, the pictures suggest a spring uncoiling, the grim acceleration of Lowry's alcoholism to its inevitable end.

The earliest pictures are of Lowry as an adolescent and young man, acting in school plays, playing the ukulele on his parents' lawn. Born in 1909, he describes an unhappy childhood—tormented by nannies, half blind for years from a neglected infection—but the pictures belie the story. Instead, they suggest the happy childhood which his family remembers. His father was a wealthy cottonbroker in Liverpool. Malcolm was the youngest of four sons. They grew up on golf courses and the seashore. Malcolm was a success in public school: he wrote sports, published short fiction, acted in plays, broke records in golf and weightlifting, and swam as impressively as his athletic, Methodist, abstemious father. Snapshots show a handsome, rugged youth with wavy brown hair, a radiant smile, and a cherubic countenance. He looked happy, even if, in some of the pictures, perhaps a bit tipsy.

(Maybe he lied about his unhappy childhood. Lowry lied a lot.)

He spent six months at sea as a deckhand—the newspapers poked fun at the idea of a rich man's son joining the working class—and then entered Cambridge. Pictures at Cambridge show a confident young man with a pipe, surrounded by admirers and other would-be writers (among them the homosexuals and communists flourishing at Cambridge, neither camp attracting Lowry). In college he was something of a legend, famous for his drinking, ukulele, and writing ability (in that order). He affected a swaggering seaman's gait copied by younger classmates. He was both the butt of jokes and considered a genius. A student magazine cartoon showed him curled up inside the body of a ukulele as if in a womb, inspired no doubt by the frequent occasions when he sprawled under tables in pubs and played the uke until passing out.

At Cambridge he talked much more about writing than he wrote. He also talked more about books than he read. In short, Malcolm

Lowry was a bit of a poseur—there were many at Cambridge in those days. During his undergraduate years, he did write the lyrics for several foxtrots—published but never popular—and also wrote his first novel, *Ultramarine*, which sufficed for a thesis to earn him, at twenty-four, a third-class tripos in English. The book is autobiographical, about storms, syphilis, and drunkenness on the high seas. The reviews were bad.

Then there are pictures of Lowry and Conrad Aiken, the poet and novelist some twenty years Lowry's senior. Lowry had read Aiken's bestseller, *Blue Horizons*, dedicated to the author's wife, whose initials were C.M.L. Lowry's initials were also C.M.L. (He hated "Clarence," his first name, and never used it.) Now comes a strange and perhaps ominous development. Convinced that *Blue Horizons* had been dedicated to *him*—Clarence Malcolm Lowry—he crossed the Atlantic to Boston where Aiken was teaching at Harvard. Aiken and Lowry got along famously. As Aiken's wife, Clarissa Lorenz, recalled, they were "both night owls, spending convivial hours at Ping-Pong and literary powwows. Their pub crawls stirred gossip . . . and upset my domestic timetable." By this she meant that both were drunk a good deal of the time and late for dinner. Once they had an arm wrestling contest over the commode in the bathroom and Aiken got a skull fracture. Nevertheless, they were mostly friends for life.

(Lowry's father, concerned about his son's drinking, paid Aiken off and on for ten years to serve as his tutor and guardian. He also paid other guardians to look after Lowry, on into Lowry's thirties. Lowry was financially dependent on his father all of his life, first receiving small allowances and then living, after his father's death, on his share of the inheritance. His writing alone could never sustain him. *Under the Volcano*, his only popular success, sold thirty thousand copies in the first few years after publication, but this provided only temporary relief from dependence on his family. Lowry's infantilism, so often noted by others, may partly have reflected the fact that, economically speaking, he retained the status of an infant until his death.)

Moving on, we see a picture of Lowry in Spain on vacation with the Aikens. He has a hangdog look and has grown fat from drinking beer. In Spain he has violent episodes while drunk, once threatening to kill Aiken. In Spain he met his first wife, Jan, an American beauty who, during their marriage, deserted him on four occasions before the divorce and was the unfaithful wife model for Yvonne in *Under the Volcano.*

Not long afterward Lowry and Jan go to Mexico where he begins writing *Under the Volcano* and stays drunk most of the time. A picture shows him smiling but troubled and obviously hung over. His drunkenness lands him in jail and his father has to send a lawyer to bail him out of jail and ultimately out of Mexico.

Then comes a remarkable series of pictures of a much changed Lowry. After Mexico he went to Los Angeles where he was declared legally incompetent and told he must leave the United States. Before leaving he met Margerie Bonner, a woman four years his senior, who was the secretary of Penny Singleton (Blondie in the movies) and an aspiring writer. She was small, vivacious, and tough. They fell in love. Lowry headed for the closest border that *wasn't* the border to Mexico and found refuge in Vancouver, British Columbia, where Margerie joined him.

Some combination of Margerie and Canada had a salubrious effect on Lowry. For a good part of fifteen years he and Margerie lived in a beach shack on Vancouver Bay, tucked in the wilderness, which he loved, and out of sight of Vancouver, which he hated. He drastically cut down on his drinking—a few beers during the day, some sipping of gin at night. This was as close to abstinence as Lowry ever got, and it was close enough to restore him to a condition of boisterous health and provide the energy to produce draft after draft of one of the greatest novels ever written.

This is all displayed beautifully in the snapshots Malcolm and Margerie took of each other during their years in Canada. Up early, swimming or doing calisthenics, Lowry became a veritable Adonis, with a weightlifter's body and the profile of Errol Flynn. Looking like tanned beachcombers, he and Margerie were always smiling. They avoided "civilization"—Vancouver—and lived in sylvan tranquility, friends of fishermen and a few other shack dwellers. Margerie wrote whodunits and sold a couple to Scribner's. More important, she collaborated with Lowry on the volcano book and everything else he wrote thereafter (continuing to collaborate after his death by editing manuscripts far too incomplete for publication). Margerie Bonner Lowry was the unnamed coauthor of *Under the Volcano,* although she insisted that Malcolm was the genius in the family and no doubt he was.

The Canadian years were the Lowrys' happiest and most productive. They called their shack in the wilderness Eridanus, meaning Eden. But then one night the shack burned down, destroying the only copy in existence of a nearly finished novel, with Lowry able to save *Under the Volcano* only by receiving serious burns which led to hospitalization. He and Margerie went off to Toronto to recover, but Eden was never truly restored, even when they returned to Vancouver Bay to build another shack.

The last pictures of Lowry in Canada show a man in trouble: flabbier, despair clearly present behind the poses and silly grins.

There are also other pictures showing Lowry looking either drunk or very hung over and with the despair always lurking behind the tan and the white teeth. These were taken on trips to Europe, Mexico, and Haiti, mostly after their shack had burned to the ground and they were searching for another Eden.

Then, with three years left to live, Lowry departed Canada for good, knowing he would never return. Pictures taken of him in 1956, one month before he died, on a holiday to the Lake Country in England, show a man at the end of his tether, empty, resigned, much older looking than his forty-seven years. Perhaps the last picture of Lowry shows Malcolm and Margerie at the door of their cottage in the village of Ripe in Sussex. Lowry looks drunk. A short time later, he drank a half bottle of gin, threatened to strangle Margerie, who left the house in a panic, and then topped off the gin with two bottles of Margerie's sleeping pills. He was found dead the next morning. The coroner's verdict was "misadventure."

The spring had uncoiled all the way.

There are also many verbal descriptions of Lowry. He showed up as a character in several novels and after his death friends were always being asked to describe what kind of man he was. The descriptions tend to be contradictory. There is much written about his moodiness and depressions, his long silences interspersed by alcohol-inspired divagations on his life, work, literature, and the world, self-adulation alternating with self-loathing. Everyone agreed he was pathologically shy and drank in part to be less shy. He was irritable during hangovers. He was self-absorbed, egocentric but not, as one critic said, conceited. All through his life he made friends, some of whom *stayed* friends despite some of the most intolerable drunken behavior imaginable. There were friends from his Cambridge days, friends who were well-known writers, one good friend who was his editor at Random House, and fishermen and other neighbors from the wilderness on the north shore of Vancouver Bay (it was still a wilderness when the Lowrys lived there). Lowry had a gift for friendship which survived his depressions, drunkenness, hangovers, and general erratic behavior.

But another aspect of Lowry's behavior is often mentioned. As a small boy he was described by a relative as "all teeth and perpetually grinning—frightfully jaunty and argumentative, rather untidy, terribly fond of talking . . . a *personality*." One ingredient of the personality was charm. Lowry had tremendous charm. It was always breaking through his gloomiest moods and most drunken moments. Recalled one Vancouver friend: "Whatever state Malc was in, he was splendidly good-natured about it. Somehow, I always thought of a fox. 'Right, they have run me to earth.' Then, in a flash, he'd be *away*, through the gents, miraculously disappearing again anywhere—anywhere to go with his fabulous mind—away from the ordinaries trying to sober him up." (The setting obviously was a pub.)

According to another friend, Lowry was a fascinating companion. "The brilliance of his mind, his extraordinary memory, the amazing range and depth of his knowledge, his fund of really funny stories in which the jokes were most often at his own expense, all astonished and captivated me as did the warmth and friendliness of his nature. . . ."

Another barhood friend remembered that the "very sight of the old bastard made me happy for five days. No bloody fooling."

Lowry, in his writings, is identified with gloom and despair but he could be the funniest of writers on occasion. *Under the Volcano* is punctuated with humor. Toward the end of his life Lowry even wrote a funny epitaph for himself:

Malcolm Lowry
Late of the Bowery

His prose was flowery
And often glowery
He lived, nightly, and drank daily
And died playing the ukulele.

His widow never had the epitaph engraved on his headstone. She probably was not feeling very giggly at the time.

Furthermore, Lowry, his friends agreed, was a *nice* man (an unusual trait in writers and geniuses). David Markson, a young friend, saw something in Lowry that accounts (Douglas Day reports) for the large number of people who were

> willing throughout his life not just to tolerate him, but actually to love him: though Lowry was usually clumsy about human relationships, if one looked closely one could see that he was capable of extraordinary affection for those in whose company he could relax. His impulses were almost always gentle and friendly—unless he were in one of his low periods, when he fairly radiated misery, and could be really cruel. At his best, he was guileless, open, and trusting: not quite puppy-like, perhaps, because the evidence of complexity, of torment overcome for the time being by cheeriness, was always there; and because there was always the self-conscious, sly trickster just beneath the surface, watching to see how well the friendly-puppy act was going over.

Cheeriness, in any case, was as much a part of Lowry's personality as despair and pathological shyness. Finally, Lowry was forever impressing people (particularly women) as vulnerable and defenseless (puppylike). As mentioned, in his undergraduate days a student magazine depicted him curled up inside the body of a ukulele. The defenseless Lowry—the Lowry who was always being taken to hospitals, sobered up, and then welcomed back to society—was described frequently by his wife Margerie. In a sad letter written to Lowry's editor after his publisher had broken the contract because Lowry simply did not send anything publishable, Margerie made one of her many pleas for compassion:

> I don't dare leave Malc very long. I haven't shown him your letter, I didn't dare. This whole business has nearly killed him. . . . He feels disgraced, cast out . . . not only his ability but even his sense of responsibility questioned etc., etc. But finally and

most importantly he is so despairingly *hurt* and heartbroken it would move a brass mule to compassion. . . . No, Albert, he doesn't want flattery (well, he likes it) but he longs for faith in him and at this stage he needs encouragement more than food. You've never seen him in the throes of creation, feeling his way, unsure (even while sure in the long run) and super super sensitive about everything. . . . You may think (and so may I for that matter) that it is immature to attach so much importance to saving face, but he has a fantastic and touchy pride and what he cannot endure is humiliation. . . . I beg you to write him an affectionate letter. . . . I am doing all I can to bolster him up, but he waits every day for some help from you. Please give him a little help, so he can get up and go on. He *has* courage. . . .

Photographs and words: these tell us what we know about Lowry's appearance and behavior. To observe his thoughts and feelings, we have an even better source: his books and letters.

His books were autobiographic, personal, subjective. The first was about his seafaring days as a schoolboy. Two are mainly about Canada or at least Lowry's version of Canada: his constantly threatened Garden of Eden. One tells about sobering up in Bellevue Hospital in New York. (If Mexico was hell for Lowry, Canada was paradise and Bellevue purgatory—an interesting analogy discussed later.) His books are dominated by two themes: what it is like to be a writer and what it is like to be an alcoholic. The themes also dominate his collected letters.

What did Lowry have to say about himself as a writer? First he was a compulsive writer. "Compulsive, yes," wrote Douglas Day, "but not *natural:* he was a writer not because words flowed effortlessly from him, but because he was damned if he were going to be anything else. To Lowry, not to write was unimaginable; not to write was death."

And write he did, from early adolescence until the day of his death. He carried small pocket notebooks with him wherever he went and left behind a Matterhorn of notes in his tiny, often illegible handwriting. He seemed never too drunk to take notes and the handwriting (not to mention ideas) often showed it.

When he was sober enough to write books and stories and poems, he wrote these also, but was never satisfied with them. He would send stories to editors and then ask to have them returned.

Under the Volcano went through four complete drafts and many rewritings before, after ten years, Lowry agreed to send it to a publisher, making the last painful alteration in a bar near Lake Ontario on Christmas Eve 1944. After four months he was still revising the galley proofs and they had to be almost forcibly removed from him.

His compulsion to write seemed matched only by his unwillingness to stop writing. His goal in revision was never contraction but always amplification. Fitzgerald divided writers into put-inners and take-outers, in which case Lowry was a *cram*-inner. When he wasn't writing poems, stories, books, and revisions thereof, or jotting down notes interminably, he was writing long, long letters.

Lowry's method of revision almost guaranteed no work would ever be completed. After his death Mrs. Lowry and Douglas Day made a heroic attempt to "finish" a novel which Day had discovered on deposit at the University of British Columbia library. Day describes the problems they faced:

> At first, the task seemed rather straightforward, textually speaking: there were . . . three distinct texts, of 383, 174, and 148 pages respectively. The three seemed to run consecutively, so that it would require only a minimal amount of housekeeping duties to provide ourselves with a respectable text. But such optimism was naïve. We found out very quickly that Lowry had *not* really worked through the three texts consecutively—that, instead, he had done an uncommon amount of backing and filling, of retracing his steps, of setting off on false starts, and even of throwing in a good deal of material that belonged elsewhere, in other novels and stories ("just for safekeeping," as he would say). In several cases, one incident existed in as many as five different versions, none immediately obvious as superior in quality to the others. Neither was it possible always—or even often—to assume blindly that the most recent version of an incident was the most finished, or even the one preferred by the author: quite frequently Lowry would write a passage, then modify it, then delete the modifications, then try others, then delete the entire passage—then reinsert it fifty pages later. There were many repetitions, and more than once we had to decide which of three identical passages, occurring in as many chapters, we were to retain. Characters were predicted who never appeared, characters appeared who had nothing much to do, and so drifted out after a few pages of embarrassed standing about.

Unintentionally, Lowry discovered an ingenious method for never finishing a piece of work. Surely, in the history of literature, no author has ever lost so many manuscripts. His first novel was lost by the publisher; a suitcase containing the manuscript was stolen from the back seat of his car. Another novel was lost in a fire. A third was lost en route to New York and found three days later. Even the Italian translation of one novel was lost and never recovered. The losses were unintentional, but they served Lowry's purpose, whatever its motivation: to avoid, at all costs, publishing a completed work.

For a compulsive writer nothing is more agonizing than a writer's block. Nobody ever complained about blocks more than Lowry or described greater agony. Here is a block described by his wife, in a letter to his editor, Albert Erskine while in Sicily:

> Malc had been trying to write you for two weeks, but the letter became more and more involved, longer, and in trying to say something, poor soul, he ended by saying nothing comprehensible, so I'm trying to figure out what he really meant to say, and say it for him. From all of which you may gather that he isn't well, and that's right he isn't, though rather better now and I have hopes. Neither Malc nor I have been able to do much work here—the *noise* has nearly driven us crazy. And Malc, of course, cannot be driven to work (in that case he just gets frantic and *can't* work) nor can he be led (he just gets balky and blank). . . . As I say, the noise. He says it sounds like a continual invasion from Mars. For another, when he tried despite noise to get down [to work], he found it still too immediately and personally anguishing, so, of course, it was going to become more and more involved, longer, and in trying etc. . . . However, it is there, and one day you'll have it, and it will be terrific.

Sometimes it was terrific. As a rule, Erskine received nothing, or nothing publishable.

To overcome his blocks Lowry engaged in rituals. Rare is the creative writer who has not done the same, but Lowry's rituals were extraordinary. During his most productive years in the Canadian wilderness, Lowry would rise early, go for a swim, then go to his desk in the shack and start to write. He wrote standing up, with his left hand turned palm up so that he eventually got calluses on his knuckles (described by a physician as "anthropoid knuckles," although this may be apocryphal). His wife, in another room, had to maintain total silence until she heard strange animallike mutterings from her husband's room, after which she could be as noisy as she wished, apparently because he had now entered the trancelike stage of creation.

Besides his blocks and benders, Lowry had another cogent reason for being unproductive: he had the compulsion to write, without very much to write *about*—except, of course, himself. His masterpiece, *Under the Volcano*, has four major characters and three of them are Malcolm Lowry. The alcoholic consul is Lowry's mature self. Hugh, the consul's half brother, is the consul in his youth. Laurulle, the consul's friend, is a mirror of the consul, as his meditations at the beginning of the novel show. *Under the Volcano* has several levels of meaning—political, religious, literary—but the book in fact is about Malcolm Lowry and little else.

Mostly it is about his alcoholism. Lowry said he had two tyrannies—the pen and the bottle—and both possessed him utterly in *Under the Volcano*. As a book by an alcoholic about alcoholism, there is no comparison anywhere in literature. *The Lost Weekend*, published three years earlier, is good, but not in the same league (although Lowry was obsessed by its greater sales, believing he had an exclusive claim to alcoholism as a literary property).

What can be said about Lowry's alcoholism that is any different from what is said about alcoholism in general?

First, Lowry engaged in long periods of controlled drinking interspersed with devastating benders. The traditional view of alcoholism held by members of Alcoholics Anonymous, among others, is that long periods of controlled drinking are incompatible with the illness. All one can say is that it sometimes happens. Faulkner was another classical alcoholic whose drinking was controlled for long stretches.

Lowry's ability to control his drinking—sometimes—may bear on the possibility that he had a *type* of alcoholism with which this is possible, a controversial subject discussed a little later.

In any case, Lowry's alcoholism fits a definition proposed by the National Council on Alcoholism: "The person with alcoholism cannot consistently predict on any drinking occasion the duration of the episode or the quantity that will be consumed." Lowry never *really* knew, when he had a drink, what would happen, nor did his apprehensive wife and friends.

People were always amazed by Lowry's recuperative powers— his ability to recover quickly from prodigious drinking bouts—as well as his formidable memory. According to the *Times Literary Supplement*, Lowry "could remember almost everything that happened during bouts of drunkenness—no alcoholic amnesia, there. . . ." Nonsense. Like all alcoholics, Lowry had blackouts, periods, often of several hours, in which he functioned almost normally and may not have seemed even very drunk, but of which he could remember nothing afterward. The consul, Lowry's alter ego in *Under the Volcano*, had blackouts. He couldn't remember going to the chapel and praying for his wife's return. He seemed in and out of blackouts through most of the book, although, as the book says, he "drank himself sober" from time to time and became totally, excruciatingly lucid.

Concerning his remarkable recuperative powers and formidable memory, one point must be made about Lowry: he was a talented actor, an exhibitionistic drunk (like Fitzgerald), a man who did a good deal of pretending to be drunk or sober. Sometimes he may not have been quite as drunk as he appeared. Drunkenness not only attracts disdain and disgust but, like any helpless state, also attracts attention, sympathy, mothering (all of which Lowry seemed inordinately in need of). Moreover, there was the "legend" to be maintained. In his teens Lowry got a reputation as a drinker and his drinking did become almost legendary at Cambridge. It was widely considered essential to his genius (a genius yet to produce a single work of art). He often carried around a ukulele in one hand and a bottle in the other. The bottle became a Lowry trademark. He seemed simultaneously ashamed of his drinking and proud of it.

Finally, there was another kind of tradition to be maintained: the tradition that great artists in Lowry's time were also great drinkers. Dylan Thomas, who personified the tradition, was a drinking companion of Lowry's when both were young. Years later they met, briefly, at the University of British Columbia, and their intoxication was avoided only by a female fan of Thomas's pulling him away for other business. Drinking and art, in twentieth-century England

and America, were widely considered inseparable. Lowry frequented working-class bars—actually the only ones he could afford—and found a sprinkling of literary drunks in most of them to reinforce his conviction that tomorrow-be-damned as long as you were an artist.

Pretense and exhibitionism notwithstanding, Lowry was a genuine alcoholic. Some critics have tended to play down his alcoholism, or at least the alcoholism of his fictional characters. Stephen Spender said that *Under the Volcano* is "no more about drinking than *King Lear* is about senility." (Some years later, in a Kansas City newspaper, a reviewer said the movie *Under the Volcano* was "no more about drinking than Hamlet was about regicide," suggesting he may have read Spender in preparation for the review.) Spender was wrong. *Under the Volcano* is a book about alcoholism. Lowry affirmed it: "The idea I cherished in my heart was to create a pioneer work in its own class and to write at last an authentic drunkard's story." When people complained about the lack of plot and characterization in his books, Lowry replied: "There are a thousand writers who can draw adequate characters till all is blue for one who can tell you anything new about hell fire." There is no doubt that hell fire, for Lowry, was alcoholism.

Except for his ability to control his drinking for long periods, Lowry's alcoholism was classical. According to classmates, he was a surreptitious drinker by age sixteen. During his six months as a deckhand on a freighter he got drunk so often that even his boozy shipmates remarked on it. In Cambridge he would stay drunk for several days at a time and became known to the Cambridge police as a disorderly drunk. His friends discovered early, as Douglas Day said, that "no one was ever really able to stop Lowry when he wanted to drink, not even the dogged Margerie [his second wife]." He would suddenly vanish for days at a time and be found "crazy drunk." His friend Peter Churchill gives an example:

> The evening before the Lowrys left had been hilarious, and, one must admit, somewhat drunken. Next morning we were due to make an early departure. Joan and I were still in bed when Margerie burst in upon us and announced with a suitably dramatic gesture that Malcolm had vanished. She had searched the house. He was gone. Edna [a hurricane] had not yet arrived, and in fact, as I remember, never did reach New York but a high wind

was blowing. I put on some clothes and went to look for Malcolm. In passing I saw that a full bottle of gin had disappeared also. I noticed that one of the low-sweeping branches of a huge Paulownia tree seemed to be swaying rather more than was accounted for by the wind. Through the mass of enormous leaves I could see Malcolm in pajamas clinging to it desperately. When he saw me he shouted, "Hang on! Here comes Edna. Don't let go!" I subdued Edna slightly by leaning heavily against the swaying branch and in a matter-of-fact tone asked Malcolm if he could lend me a razor blade as all mine seemed to be blunt. Edna forgotten, he followed me into the house and duly found me a razor blade.

He always had excuses for drinking: the loss of a manuscript, a story rejected, unhappy love, the "sterility of existence." One of his favorite excuses was that people encouraged him to drink and then condemned him for becoming drunk. This was undoubtedly true in the pub-crawling ebullience of his college days and later in life with the heavy-drinking New York literary crowd. He particularly blamed the Mexicans for encouraging him to drink and then slapping him in jail when he got drunk.

In his thirties Lowry was drinking shaving lotion and other non-beverage forms of alcohol when alcohol wasn't available, which comes close to reaching bottom, as AA members put it, and hospitalizations became inevitable. His first was at Bellevue Hospital in New York. Admissions increased in frequency as he got older. Toward the end of his life a lobotomy was considered, and on two occasions he underwent aversion therapy in London hospitals. (Aversion therapy consists of giving a vomiting-inducing drug whenever the patient drinks so that he associates vomiting with alcohol and presumably will stop drinking because the sight or taste of alcohol makes him nauseated. Aversion therapy didn't work; Lowry went straight from hospital to pub both times.)

In any case, vomiting was nothing novel for Lowry: he vomited blood on several occasions, presumably from gastritis. He also had grand-mal seizures and episodes of delirium tremens. He took pills, mainly barbiturates, in an attempt to reduce his drinking, but alcohol remained his "poison of choice" for life. He was sometimes violent when drunk, physically attacking his wife, and died by an act of violence against himself. A coroner called his death a misadventure, but the evidence points to suicide. Although drunk when he swallowed forty to fifty tablets of sodium amytal, he hid the containers afterward. Even with alcohol-impaired judgment, it is hard to interpret this as accidental. Swallowing fifty tablets of anything requires dedication.

The fact is that Lowry, like many severe alcoholics, was suicidal in the advanced stage of his illness. A quarter of the suicides by men over thirty-five in the United States are alcoholic. Lowry, in his role as consul, was murdered in the book but he seemed to be asking for it. At one point he could have walked out of the bar and saved his life, but he stayed for another drink. "He had, in fact, chosen to die," concludes one critic. Drunkenness alone wouldn't kill the consul so he invited murder, just as Lowry needed a combination of alcohol and barbiturates to do the job.

Under the Volcano is a manual on alcoholism. "By the time we finish the novel," Stephen Spender writes, "we know how a drunk thinks and feels, walks and lies down, and we experience not only the befuddledness of drinking but also its moments of translucent clairvoyance." Art Hill, in the autumn 1974 issue of *Canadian Literature*, extracted from the book some salient features of alcoholism and did it so eloquently that his remarks bear repeating.

First, there is the alcoholics' talent for self-deception. Hill writes:

> Alcoholics lie. It is intrinsic. They lie to their friends, they lie to themselves, they even lie to other alcoholics. Non-addicted drinkers often brag about how much they drink; alcoholics almost always minimize it. This is not to say that the alcoholic is basically dishonest. He may be a model of virtue in all things, except where his drinking is concerned. But this is misleading, because almost every decision an alcoholic makes is influenced by its possible effect on his ability to get a drink, now or two weeks hence.
>
> To illustrate: given a choice of two parties to attend at some future date, the alcoholic will, within seconds, weigh half a dozen factors quite beyond the imagination of the normal person. The possible congeniality of the company may *not* be one of them. He may, in fact, prefer to spend the evening with people he doesn't much like. If the prospective host is lavish with his spirits, that will obviously weigh in his favor. But more important is his *style* of entertaining. Does he urge people to pour their own drinks? Does he leave the liquor around where anyone can get at it? Is the

drink-mixing spot out of sight of the room where the guests congregate? Do the host and hostess tend to over-drink (which draws attention away from others who do)? The list of possible questions is unlimited, but the experienced alcoholic will consider all of them. If the signs are favorable, he will get three times as much to drink as the average guest, without anyone's seeing him. If he is plainly very drunk at the end of the evening, he will be put down as one of those unfortunate people who can't hold their liquor, at least by those who don't know him. (The "invisible" drink is of course the source of the persistent notion that alcoholics regularly get roaring drunk on three or four drinks.)

If all this seems exaggerated, it is not. If it seems ludicrous, well, it is. The total dedication of a good mind to such a trivial pursuit is patently ridiculous. But it's deadly serious to the millions of good minds so dedicated at this moment.

Then there is the deferred-drink gambit:

. . . it is one more affliction of the alcoholic that he is always ashamed of his drinking. This is why, drunk or sober, he maintains the fiction that he could drink moderately, and surely will next time. He does not, *ever,* consider stopping until he faces the fact that moderation is not within his power.

One device the alcoholic uses to enforce the self-delusion that he doesn't "need" the drink is the tactic of spurious indifference. *Under the Volcano* is practically a textbook in the use of this gambit, which is absurdly simple. Given a drink after a period of abstinence (of any length), the alcoholic simply delays drinking it. . . . Deferring the moment of consumption supports the belief that it will be voluntary. . . .

Alcoholism is a full-time job. It destroys other interests:

Alcoholics are spectators. Their single hobby leaves no time for other avocations. . . .

The principal reason for his spectator status, though, is simply that the recreational activities of others get them out of the way so he can drink unobserved. This is why the alcoholic is always urging others to "have some fun" . . . go away, in short, and leave him to his own miserable fun.

Hill on the double-entry drink-counting system:

Secret drinking leads inevitably to the practice of drink count-
ing, which, as done by the alcoholic, has no relation to standard
arithmetic. Lowry expounds this point deftly, as the three prin-
cipals sit down to eat at the Ofélia. The Consul is, at first, in a
jovial mood. He has had, by alcoholic count, very little to drink—
because the others did not see him drink the eight or nine secret
mescals. He has sworn Cervantes, the bartender, to silence. Still,
Hugh and Yvonne seem to suspect. Cervantes must have told on
him. . . . According to his double-entry drink-counting system,
he has been observing a code of conduct so nearly puritanical that
he really ought to let down a bit and have a drink. He is probably
surprised they don't suggest it. The fact that they can see he is
drunk does not occur to him. By *his* count, he is obviously sober
in *their* eyes.

No one understands:

No one who is not an alcoholic can ever understand the alcoholic's need to drink. He does not understand it himself, but he
knows what it *feels* like, something no "outsider" can know. . . .

There is a story about Ronald Reagan which beautifully confirms
the point Hill is making. Reagan, while president of the Screen
Guild, repaired to a bar after a meeting with two vice presidents,
Dana Andrews and William Holden. Both Andrews and Holden
were to become serious alcoholics, but this was not known at the
time. The three of them had a drink. Then Andrews and Holden
waved frantically at a waitress, asking for a refill.

"But you just *had* a drink," says Reagan. Reagan is not an alcoholic and had no notion of an alcoholic's needs. Well, after all, if
three people sat down and had a chicken dinner and then two of
them ordered a *second* chicken dinner . . . you'd *surely* be puzzled.
Reagan was.

Lowry wrote not only the best book about alcoholism but also the
best descriptions of a rather rare manifestation of alcoholism, delirium tremens. Delirium tremens is different from simple alcohol
withdrawal. The latter is manifested by shakes, sweating, insomnia, and occasional transient hallucinations. Delirium tremens

includes shakes—the tremens part—and also delirium, a nightmarish condition in which the victim is disoriented and delusional, and has vivid, nonstop, usually frightening hallucinations.

In *Under the Volcano* it is hard to tell when the consul is hallucinating and when he is not. The whole book has a hallucinatory quality. One beautiful example of hallucinations can be viewed in John Huston's movie version of *Under the Volcano* wherein Albert Finney, after a night of drinking, is interrupted in a rambling tale by his long-absent wife, Yvonne, unexpectedly walking into the bar. Looking over his shoulder, Finney sees her, pauses, then returns to his story. He keeps looking back over his shoulder and returning to his story until, finally, he realizes that Yvonne is not a hallucination (of the kind he is so familiar with) but actually Yvonne. (Finney's portrayal of an alcoholic in his cups will probably never be surpassed; the scene showing him trying to decide whether he is having a hallucination is so utterly convincing that even the sanest of nonalcoholics may recognize that that is the way it probably is.)

In his late twenties Lowry spent ten days in Bellevue Hospital in New York and then spent twenty years trying to describe the experience, resulting in one of his most brilliant works, the posthumously published *Lunar Caustic*. Lowry had delirium tremens in Bellevue and his description of DTs is pure art:

> The man awoke certain that he was on a ship. If not, where did those isolated clangings come from, those sounds of iron on iron? He recognized the crunch of water pouring over the scuttle, the heavy tramp of feet on the deck above, the steady *Frère Jacques*: *Frère Jacques* of the engines. He was on a ship, taking him back to England, which he never should have left in the first place. Now he was conscious of his racked, trembling, malodorous body. Daylight sent probes of agony against his eyelids. Opening them, he saw three negro sailors vigorously washing down the deck. He shut his eyes again. Impossible, he thought. . . .
>
> As the day grew, the noise became more ghastly: what sounded like a railway seemed to be running just over the ceiling. Another night came. The noise grew worse and, stranger yet, the crew kept multiplying. More and more men, bruised, wounded, and always drunk, were hurled down the alley by petty officers to lie face downward, screaming or suddenly asleep on their hard bunks.

He was awake. What had he done last night? Nothing at all, perhaps, yet remorse tore at his vitals. He needed a drink desperately. He did not know whether his eyes were closed or open. Horrid shapes plunged out of the blankness, gibbering, rubbing their bristles against his face, but he couldn't move. Something had got under his bed too, a bear that kept trying to get up. Voices, a prosopopoeia of voices, murmured in his ears, ebbed away, murmured again, cackled, shrieked, cajoled; voices pleading with him to stop drinking, to die and be damned. Thronged, dreadful shadows came close, were snatched away. A cataract of water was pouring through the wall, filling the room. A red hand gesticulated, prodded him: over a ravaged mountain side a swift stream was carrying with it legless bodies yelling out of great eye-sockets, in which were broken teeth. Music mounted to a screech, subsided. On a tumbled bloodstained bed in a house whose face was blasted away a large scorpion was gravely raping a one-armed negress. His wife appeared, tears streaming down her face, pitying, only to be instantly transformed into Richard III, who sprang forward to smother him.

Oh, Lowry was an alcoholic all right!

Lowry's wife, and others, often called his alcoholism secondary. Secondary to what?

In the scientific literature on alcoholism, the illness *is* sometimes divided into primary and secondary. "Primary" means the illness develops inexplicably—out of the blue—in a formerly healthy individual. "Secondary" means the opposite: a person with a preexistent psychiatric illness drinks too much and the reason is the preexistent illness.

Nowadays, primary alcoholism is sometimes equated with "familial" alcoholism. This is based on the fact that some alcoholics have alcoholism in the family and others do not, and there seem to be clinical differences between the two types. The familial alcoholic starts drinking at an earlier age and has a particularly malignant form of alcoholism, but once he stops drinking, there seems to be nothing else psychiatrically wrong with him. Alcoholics *without* a family history of alcoholism are more likely to have another psychiatric disorder. They also are more likely to sustain long periods of controlled drinking than is the familial alcoholic. Curing secondary alcoholism means first curing the psychiatric disorder which gave rise to it.

In none of the accounts of the Lowry family is there any mention of alcoholism. His father was a teetotaler who died of cirrhosis of the liver. This rather amused Malcolm, whose liver was always declared normal. This was about the only manifestation of alcoholism spared Lowry, but only some 10 percent of severe alcoholics develop cirrhosis and Lowry was one of the fortunate majority. In any case, based on the public record, Lowry had a nonfamilial form of alcoholism, which, if true, meant his alcoholism could indeed be considered secondary and caused by another psychiatric disorder. (If so, this would explain why he could maintain long periods of controlled drinking, but remember that Faulkner also controlled his drinking for fairly long periods and no other writer in this book had *more* alcoholism in the family than did Faulkner. Science doesn't have all the answers yet.)

Therefore, presuming Lowry's alcoholism was caused by another disorder, what was the disorder?

The leading candidate, in the view of most observers, was depression. He had frequent mood swings dating from adolescence, and sometimes the blackest of depressions. He attempted suicide several times before succeeding. He was frequently self-depreciatory, as are depressed persons, describing himself as "uncultured, unobservant . . . ignorant . . . lacking nearly all the qualities you normally associate with a writer . . . a person both human and pathetically inhuman at once."

One problem with the diagnosis of depression is that Lowry never stopped drinking through his adult life and was very often drunk or hung over. Alcohol is a toxin. Alcoholics are *always* depressed, both during the lachrymose stage of drunkenness and particularly on the morning after. Alcoholics experience remorse, guilt, insomnia, anorexia, suicidal thoughts, loss of interest in other activities—in short, all the symptoms of depression. A few days or weeks after an alcoholic stops drinking the symptoms often go away, suggesting they were caused by alcohol.

Even those alcoholics who commit suicide do not often show signs of depression when not drinking. There is a syndrome called "alcoholic dysphoria" which afflicts some drinkers who become so acutely depressed after drinking that suicide seems the only way to stop the pain.

"You cannot know the sadness of my life," says the consul to Yvonne. Did the sadness make him drink? Or did drinking make him sad? Or both? Lowry doesn't hazard a guess.

Recent evidence suggests that many alcoholics, perhaps one-third, suffer severe phobias which precede their heavy drinking and indeed may promote the drinking. Lowry had many phobias. He wouldn't eat fish because he was afraid of choking on the bones. He once developed a phobia about picking up his fountain pen. He always sat at the back of buses and airplanes because he didn't like people looking at him. He became absolutely paralyzed at any social gathering, rendered mute, until he had a few drinks. He had a particular fear of authority, dating perhaps from his fear of an intimidating father, reinforced by unpleasant experiences of going through customs into various countries. This fear of "people in charge," according to Art Hill, "says as much about the potential or incipient alcoholic as could ever be said in so compact a phrase." Lowry feared "not just the policeman or the boss, but the room clerk, the usher, the stranger on the telephone (who must be in charge of something, or one would not be talking to him)."

Of all his phobias, the most severe and lifelong was a fear of venereal disease. One of his Cambridge friends called him a "true syphilophobe" who talked about syphilis so much that people thought he had it. As Hill points out, syphilis in those prepenicillin days was a far more terrifying disease than it is now, almost akin to AIDS in its capacity to inspire fear.

This leads to an interesting but quite unprovable theory about why Lowry *really* drank. As randy as any other adolescent, he yearned for sex but was so terrified of contracting venereal disease that he avoided girls and drank instead. Alcohol, in short, became a substitute for sex—just as in Ireland, in earlier days, parents thought it was a fine thing for young men to get drunk in pubs because at least they wouldn't be outdoors seducing Irish maidens.

The sources of Lowry's syphilophobia are obvious: there was a museum in Liverpool showing diseased organs in syphilitic victims. His father warned him interminably about VD. As a schoolboy sailing on a freighter he had frequent occasions to observe the ravages of syphilis and gonorrhea in his shipmates. When *they* went ashore to have sex, Lowry went ashore to get drunk. It is not clear from his letters or biography when he first had sexual intercourse but there are suggestions that he was a frequent masturbator and a virgin until sometime in his twenties.

Ironically, alcohol helped Lowry avoid sex and therefore syphilis, but it also helped him to avoid sex in a way he had not anticipated: he was often impotent. Alcohol, in Shakespeare's famous phrase, both "provokes and unprovokes; it provokes the desire but it takes away the performance." Lowry's first wife blamed Lowry for her frequent infidelities: *he* couldn't perform so she turned elsewhere. His sex life with his second wife, particularly in Canada where the drinking was greatly moderated, was reportedly adequate. But one reason Margerie hated to see him get drunk was that she knew their sex life would suffer. That he (sober) had sex with his wives at all probably reflects his belief that they were fairly safe risks as far as syphilis was concerned. Unlike his friend Dylan Thomas, Lowry was not a womanizer. Syphilophobia may be one of the most effective birth-control measures ever devised. (The Lowrys, incidentally, never had a child.)

The syphilis-alcoholism theory receives support—probably as dubious as any support could possibly be—from something Lowry mumbled while delirious at Bellevue: "Hullo, father, return to the presexual revives the necessity for nutrition." You *could* interpret this as meaning that alcoholism had rendered Lowry "presexual," meaning he needn't worry about VD. Far-fetched but no more far-fetched than some psychoanalysts' interpretations of a psychotic's ravings.

There is evidence that toward the end of his life Lowry was beginning to have brain damage. He had trouble tying his tie and putting on his socks, and handling a knife or fork. Even when sober he at times needed his wife to light his cigarettes because he said he couldn't move his fingers. (Was this because of a finger-moving phobia? Because of damage to the nervous system? Or because of catatonia—a possibility discussed a little later.) He also was having difficulty with his vision and very likely had a condition called alcohol/tobacco amblyopia. Lowry, a heavy smoker, undoubtedly had elevated cyanide levels in his blood, a condition believed responsible for visual failure in heavy-smoking alcoholics.

Lowry, in his last years, would be described by many psychiatrists as a man with alcoholic deterioration. Perhaps. According to his wife, his mind was clear and his nervous system intact during most of the sober periods preceding his death.

There is still a final diagnostic possibility to be considered and that is schizophrenia.

Lowry had at least some of the symptoms of schizophrenia, although, like depression, symptoms of schizophrenia can also be caused by alcohol. He seems to have undergone a rather marked personality change in adolescence. No longer the cheerful, bubbly, talkative child, he had long moments of silence and became painfully shy in social gatherings. He decided to be a writer: a solitary activity. His dress deteriorated; he sometimes buried his socks rather than wash them, was often dirty, disheveled, and unshaven, and wrapped a necktie around his waist to hold up baggy pants. Personality changes of this type are characteristic of early schizophrenia, but of course many nonschizophrenics have "identity crises" in adolescence and behave peculiarly by adult middle-class standards. (Maybe Lowry was just an early hippie.)

Nevertheless, by his late teens more ominous symptoms were appearing. As mentioned earlier, he crossed the Atlantic to visit Conrad Aiken because he felt, delusionally, that Aiken had dedicated a novel to him. In his early twenties he had another apparent delusion. He found two magazines on a table where there had previously been one and concluded that a thief had broken into the house and left a magazine on the table: hardly credible, according to Aiken, who was there at the time.

And then Lowry began having recurrent persecutory delusions which persisted through his life, although one can never quite be certain whether they occurred when he was drinking or sober. They consisted mainly of delusions that people were watching and following him. One of the first times a friend noticed that Lowry's eccentricity represented something more than "just youthful high spirits" occurred at a swimming party:

> He had a terrible obsession that he was being shadowed by a male nurse whom his family had put on him, and he said one day, "I swam out three miles in Torbay this morning and I turned over to float, and, do you know, he was following me." And we said, "But where is he?" He said, "I don't know. He just appears and disappears."

Years later he wrote his poet friend John Davenport: "Everywhere I go I am pursued and even now, as I write, no less than five policemen are watching me." He was in Mexico at the time and in trouble with the police because of frequent drunkenness, but Davenport, at least, considered the report bizarre.

Still later, sitting in a Mexican bar, he wrote a friend saying he was in the bar because "there is much hostility in my hotel" and goes on as follows:

> I am trying to do some work here but my life is so circum-scribed by detectives who walk up and down the street and stand at the street corner as though there were nothing better to do than to spy on a man who is unable to do anything anyway and never had intentions of doing anything but be good and love and help where help was necessary that I am rapidly losing my mind. It is not drink that does this. . . . If I do not drink now a certain amount there seems no possible doubt that I shall have a nervous breakdown.

Lowry devoutly believed that a "certain amount" of alcohol was necessary to prevent nervous breakdowns. His intention, he said, was to drink *through* a breakdown, instead of *into* a breakdown. On the several occasions when he was hospitalized for depression and not merely to sober up, he attributed his breakdowns to inability to obtain alcohol.

This, of course, could be one more excuse for drinking. Conceivably, however, if Lowry's psychiatric problem *was* schizophrenia, the alcohol may indeed have had a therapeutic, or Thorazine-like, effect. Alcohol functions as a kind of filter for the nervous system, and the schizophrenic, according to some theories, is a person lacking filters. The world is too much for the schizophrenic. Lacking filters, he drowns in stimuli.

There are suggestions that Lowry drowned in stimuli. He was eternally hypervigilant, constantly observant of his mental contents and his surroundings. Constant note taking may have been one way in which he attempted to channel or check the flood of stimuli, control it, at least give it meaning. He was always seeking for meaning in things, always a searcher for symbols. Nobody else better describes this than Lowry himself, in *Under the Volcano*; at one point the consul, standing at a bar, ponders real life versus symbolic life:

Life was a forest of symbols, was it, Baudelaire had said? But, it occurred to him, even before the forest, if there were such a thing as "before," were there not still the symbols? Yes, before! Before you knew anything about life, you had the symbols. It was with symbols that you started. From them you progressed to something else. Life was indeed what you made of the symbols and, the less you made of life the more symbols you got. And the more you tried to comprehend them, confusing what life was, with the necessity for this comprehension, *the more they multiplied. And the more they multiplied, that is, disintegrated into still more and more symbols which in the first place never had the slightest intention of meaning anything, let alone of being understood,* just like human beings in short, the more they liked it, until, in the end, *life itself . . . fluttered away abruptly, leaving an abstraction behind.* [Italics added.]

This passage (which could have been lifted verbatim from the case history of a schizophrenic) begins by seeking symbols, connections, in order to understand life. "But," as Douglas Day notes, "if one is not wary, he is caught up in the symbols themselves, which, after all, obscure life more than they illuminate it. And the more one is caught up in them, the more the symbols proliferate, until life is totally gone, leaving behind it a fantastically spun-out web of symbols, beautiful perhaps, but after all only a network of empty abstractions."

Day, having read so much Lowry, here almost sounds like Lowry but he takes too much for granted. When he says a person may be victimized by symbols, if unwary, he overlooks the possibility that some people have no choice: they *cannot* control the beautiful abstractions, wary or not. Schizophrenics lack precisely such control. Lowry may have lacked it. His inability to pick up a pen, his clumsiness, his other difficulties with voluntary movement, *may* have represented a form of catatonia, which is a manifestation of schizophrenia.

He also displayed ambivalence, another symptom of schizophrenia, captured brilliantly in a prayer by the consul (Lowry) to an image of the Virgin:

Please let me make her [Yvonne] happy, deliver me from this dreadful tyranny of self. I have sunk low. Let me sink lower still, that I may know the truth. Teach me to love again, to love life. Where is love? Let me truly suffer. Give me back my purity, the knowledge of the Mysteries, that I have betrayed and lost. . . . Let me be truly lonely, that I may honestly pray. Let us be happy again somewhere, if it's only together, if it's only out of this terrible world. "Destroy the world!" he cried in his heart.

As Spender points out, when he prays to be reconciled with Yvonne he also prays to be alone, and when he wants to rise he asks that he may sink still lower. That's ambivalence!

More than once he gives hints of suffering "delusions of influence" (a psychiatric term), insisting that, instead of writing, he was being *written*. (A Lowryan metaphor? Possibly. Possibly not.)

Alcoholism, he said, comes from being "baffled" by existence. No one is more baffled by existence than a schizophrenic incapable of distinguishing dreams from reality. When Lowry talks about the "dreadful tyranny of self," he is describing autism, another schizophrenic symptom, although, again, it simply may be Lowry waxing poetic.

Even his hatreds—the hatreds of fear and bafflement—had a schizophrenic quality, as one of his (autobiographic) novels, *Ultramarine*, bears out:

. . . out of fears grew wild hatreds, great unreasoning esemplastic hatreds: hatred of people who looked at him so strangely in the street; long-forgotten hatreds of schoolmates who'd persecuted him about his eyes at school; hatred of the day that ever gave him birth to be the suffering creature that he was, hatred of a world where your house burned down with no reason, hatred of himself, and out of all this hatred did not grow sleep.

Schizophrenics do not usually commit violence, but when they do—when they shoot a president or kill a rock star—the hatred they describe in their diaries (the inevitable diaries) expresses hatreds as unreasoning and "esemplastic" as those described by Malcolm Lowry. As she described in a letter to John Davenport, Margerie knew the hatreds well:

The tragic fact is that Malcolm is losing his mind and now it is going quickly so that one can see the change from week to week. He has periods of apparent calm and brilliance followed by periods of blackness. And he is becoming actively dangerous: first to himself and me but now more savage to anyone who crosses him in any way. Of course when he drinks it becomes intensely aggravated.

Again . . . when he drinks. She too had trouble knowing what was booze and what wasn't.

The strongest evidence of schizophrenia still probably consists of the apparently chronic persecutory delusions, *not* a typical manifestation of alcoholism. The alcohol, the note taking, letter writing, and the novels which he *refused* to finish may all have been filters: attempts to organize an impossibly disordered mental life.

On the other hand, it may have been only the drinking. As a friend said, slightly exaggerating, Lowry was "slightly slozzled all the time" and alcoholism is a great mimicker of psychiatric illness, even schizophrenia.

"With Lowry," Stephen Spender wrote, "one is never far away from the thought that although there is an illness there may also be a cure." Despite everything, Lowry was incurably optimistic. (More evidence, perhaps, against the depression theory of his alcoholism.) Incredibly, the last story he ever wrote, "Forest Path to the Spring," was upbeat: it had a happy ending. He believed in hell, had experienced hell, had *sought* hell—"Hell is my natural habitat," says the consul—but he believed just as strongly in salvation. Lowry was a religious man, not the churchgoing type but a mystic who believed in demons, heaven and hell, divine (or at least magical) intervention in human affairs. He seemed to feel that God, like Lowry himself, was basically good-natured and meant well.

Hell was Mexico—"the most Christ-awful place in the world . . . a sort of Moloch that feasts on suffering souls." New York was also hell—"a bad place to get on the right side of despair." Bellevue Hospital, on the other hand, was purgatory, a place where redemption was possible.

Paradise, for Lowry, was Canada, or what Canada represented, or, more precisely, what the Canadian wilderness represented. First there were few people and the ones who were there were uneducated, ordinary, "humble" people who didn't challenge Lowry, who weren't in the race to be the world's greatest writer. For a man with major social phobias, wilderness is truly salvation.

Lowry may have remembered, dimly, a similar paradise in his childhood. He grew up in idyllic surroundings, in the pleasant Cheshire countryside facing the broad river that came in from the sea, across which, on clear days, he could see the mountains in Wales. At some point in his childhood it ceased being a paradise for Lowry (if it ever was). It probably happened when life became competitive. His father was an intensely competitive man who demanded much of his sons, including financial success and success in athletics. For a time, in his school days, Lowry was competitive; he was the schoolboy golf champion of England and excelled at swimming and other sports. But after all the success he lost the competitive spirit. He barely got a degree at Cambridge, gave up golf, and became a virtual recluse, except when he drank and could tolerate people.

In any case, it is possible to imagine Lowry as having a paradise-lost syndrome: to view his permanent departure from the comfortable Lowry home and his restless wanderings as a kind of exile, a search for a lost Eden. If this has any truth at all, he found the Eden in British Columbia, in the wilderness, on the bay.

But across the bay, barely ten miles away, was trouble, bad trouble. The Vancouver taxpayers were forever threatening to evict the squatters with their untaxed shacks on the bay. They were an eyesore. They should be torn down, perhaps replaced with an amusement park. Vancouver was spreading. Eventually urban sprawl would wipe out the shacks, but some Vancouverians wanted faster action. The Lowrys lived in constant dread that they would be evicted from paradise. Lowry once attributed alcoholism to the "ugliness and sterility of existence *sold* to people" like himself. Writing to a friend, he probably had Vancouver in mind, a city

> composed of dilapidated half-skyscrapers, at different levels, some with all kinds of scrap iron, even broken airplanes, on their roofs, others being moldy stock exchange buildings, new beer parlors crawling with verminous light even in mid-afternoon and resembling gigantic emerald-lit public lavatories for both sexes, masonries containing English tea-shoppes . . . totem pole factories, drapers' shops with the best Scotch tweed and opium dens in the basement. . . .

"Anyone who had ever really been in Hell," Lowry concludes, "must have given [Vancouver] a nod of recognition." As with his other hells—Mexico and New York—a sober Lowry could hardly tolerate Vancouver.

So he stayed as much as possible in the shack, still more or less optimistic.

Besides, it was all so lovely. In winter:

> The wintry landscape could be beautiful on these rare short days of sunlight and frostflowers, with crystal casing on the slender branches of birches and vine-leaved maples, diamond drops on the tassels of the spruces, and the bright frosted foliage of the evergreens. The frost melted on our porch in stripes, leaving a pattern against the wet black wood like a richly beaded cape flung out, on which our little cat tripped about with cold dainty paws and then sat hunched outside on the windowsill with his tail curled round his feet.

In spring,

> The very quality of the light was different, the pale green, green and gold dappled light that comes when the leaves are very small, for later, in summer with the leaves full out, the green is darker and the path darker and deeply shady. But now there was this delicate light and greenness everywhere, the beauty of light on the feminine leaves of vine-leaved maples and the young leaves of the alders shining in sunlight like stars of dogwood blossoms, green overhead and underfoot where plants were rushing up and there were the little beginnings of wild flowers that would be, my wife said, spring beauties, starflowers, wild bleeding hearts, saxifrage and bronze bells.

"Forest Path to the Spring," his last story, had been intended to be the final section of a cycle of books called *Voyage That Never Ends*, conceived when he was a young man. The story is about a jazz composer (Lowry) who lives in a beach shack with his wife (Margerie) in British Columbia. They are very happy. The shack burns down, destroying a jazz masterpiece, but they bravely build another shack and he continues working. Their life is idyllic. The air is clean. The swimming is good. There is much exercise for both of them (exercise for Lowry was always the antithesis of drinking, almost an antidote for drinking, which unfortunately never worked for very long).

There is always the threat, of course, that this paradise too will . lost, by eviction, natural catastrophe, or some other demonic force. The threat is symbolized by a cougar that confronts the story's hero on the path to the spring. Lowry tells the cougar to go away, and it does. This gives him confidence. The cougar represents "something on the path that had seemed ready, on every side, to spring out of our paradise at us." But he has mastered the cougar; he can now face the other fears.

Living in the wilderness, Lowry said, he could be a "simple fool." What did he mean by this? The answer may help us solve the problem of his illness: Was it simply alcoholism or was there something else wrong, as noted earlier, perhaps schizophrenia?

Lowry was a bad editor, both of his books and of sensations and symbols. Schizophrenic or not, he lacked filters. It was as if he were born without a skin, as someone once said. By isolating himself in a forest, he at least escaped social stimuli—the tumultuous demanding presence of other people. (Lowry shared Sartre's sentiment, "Hell is people.")

Lowry was forever converting his experiences into symbols; everything always had a meaning. *Under the Volcano* consists of layer upon layer of meaning. His mind was awash in symbols. In the opinion of Douglas Day, the wilderness was therapeutic for Lowry, as therapeutic as alcohol, without the hangover. He was a simple fool but a wise fool, for what he had learned over the years was that he and his wife had reached

> a region where such words as spring, water, houses, trees, vines, laurels, mountains, wolves, bay, roses, beach, islands, forest, tides and deer and snow and fire, had realized their true being, or had their source: and as these words on a page once stood merely to what they symbolized, so did the reality we knew now stand to something else beyond that symbolized or reflected: it was as if we were clothed in the kind of reality which before we saw only at a distance. . . . ["Forest Path to the Spring"]

Day then makes a striking and original point:

Here it all at last was, the experience of that which Lowry all his life had known was there, but had been unable quite to perceive: that what one needs to know about reality is only that it is real. Here are . . . *things,* fully realized in their existential *thingness;* here are, at last, no empty abstractions, no frenzied need to symbolize, no whirling cerebral chaos. Here is only a quiet, green world on the edge of the life-bringing sea, where the Lowryan man may protect his fragile self, love his wife, and deal reverently and perhaps a little humorously with the *things* that surround him.

Schizophrenics are said to be "out of touch with reality." Day says the simple life in the wilderness brought Lowry closer to reality, reducing his need for symbols, for filters, for alcohol.

It is an interesting idea.

Bibliographical Note

Conrad Knickerbocker, the man originally assigned to write Malcolm Lowry's biography, committed suicide in 1966. He had been making notes and conducting interviews for two years. His notes were made available to the young American scholar Douglas Day. Lowry's second wife, Margerie, cooperated fully with Day. He received permission to quote from unpublished letters, notebooks, and diaries and obviously spent many hours with Mrs. Lowry reviewing the eighteen years of the Lowrys' marriage. He also, clearly, read everything written by Lowry as well as everything about him and interviewed scores of friends and acquaintances. Day's well-written biography, *Malcolm Lowry: A Biography* (New York: Oxford University Press, 1973), with photographs, constitutes the best and most comprehensive work available on the subject.

A much smaller biography, written with charm and compassion, is *Malcolm Lowry: His Art and Early Life* by M.C. Bradbrook, who was mistress of Girton College and professor of English at Cambridge University when her book appeared in 1974. She was the same age as Lowry, had been born and raised in the same town, and was at Cambridge when Lowry was there. She brings to the book an insider's view of Wirral, Cheshire, where she and Lowry were children, and also of the intellectual ferment at Cambridge in the late twenties and early thirties when bright young men who would later become poets, novelists, politicians—and communists—had picnics on the lawn of J.B.S. Haldane.

When John Huston's movie *Under the Volcano* was released in 1984, it resulted in a new paperback edition of the novel *Under the Volcano* (New York: New American Library, 1984) with an introduction by Stephen Spender. It is very well done. The introduction by Douglas Day to *Dark as the Grave Wherein My Friend Is Laid*—the uncompleted novel he found in the archives at the University of British Columbia—is also excellent (New York: New American Library, 1968). In Lowry's posthumous collection of short stories called *Hear Us O Lord from Heaven Thy Dwelling Place* are such stories as "Under the Panama" and "The Forest Path to the Spring" (New York: Lippincott, 1961).

Canadian Literature, edited for many years by George Woodstock, has published many articles about Lowry, some first-rate. The journal has also published bibliographies and supplements compiled by Lowry's friend Earl Birney and Mrs. Lowry. The autumn 1974 issue of *Canadian Literature* includes a wise and penetrating article by Art Hill about Lowry's alcoholism. I have long admired Mr. Hill's article and have tried to contact him to discuss it with him, but without success.

In the June 1970 issue of *Atlantic*, Clarissa Lorenz tells about Lowry's belief that Conrad Aiken's novel *Blue Horizons* had been dedicated to him, which if true can only be interpreted as a delusion. Since it is not mentioned in other works on Lowry, one is entitled to some skepticism about its accuracy.

Other sources include Thomas B. Gilmore's "The Place of Hallucinations in *Under the Volcano,*" *Contemporary Literature* 23 (1982); *Malcolm Lowry: A Preface to His Fiction* by Richard K. Cross (Chicago: University of Chicago Press, 1980); *the Art of Malcolm Lowry,* edited by Anne Smith (New York: Vision Press, 1978); Malcolm Lowry's *Volcano: Myth, Symbol, Meaning* (New York: Times Books, 1978); *Malcolm Lowry's Infernal Paradise* by Christopher Dorosz (Uppsala, Sweden, 1976).

Lowry's avidity for symbols makes his work fair game for Ph.D. thesis writers, and a number have been published examining Homeric parallels in the novel, concepts from Jung, Spengler, Freud, Frazer, Spinoza, and Shelley, Oriental metaphysics, and the philosophical idealism of George Berkeley, not to mention references to Aiken (his mentor), Joyce, Dante, Aztec mythology, Elizabethan poetry, Swedenborg, and German expressionist films.

The list is not complete. Ideally, but beyond the grasp of most, the reader should be familiar with all the symbols and esoterica to comprehend completely the works of Malcolm Lowry. Fortunately, this is entirely unnecessary to enjoy his work.

9

NOTES ON AN EPIDEMIC

Of course, you're a rummy . . .
but no more than most good writers are.

Hemingway to Fitzgerald

Drinking is the writer's vice.

Fitzgerald

Alcoholism is unevenly distributed among groups. More men than women are alcoholic, more Irishmen than Jews, more bartenders than bishops. The group, however, with perhaps a higher rate of alcoholism than any other consists of famous American writers.

Whether, as Hemingway said, most good writers are alcoholic is uncertain, but apparently a large number are. Compile a list of well-known American writers of the past century and quite possibly one-third to one-half could be considered alcoholic.

In the introduction I use the word *epidemic* to describe the problem. Based on the facts, the word seems to fit. Accepting this, we can ask five questions:

1. Did the epidemic mainly involve American writers?
2. Did it chiefly occur in the first half of the twentieth century? What about the second half?
3. Did the epidemic involve creative people in the other arts?
4. Did it mainly involve well-known writers?
5. Did it involve specifically alcohol, or were other drugs also abused?

After trying to answer these questions, one then comes to the ultimate question: *Why?*

Questions

1. *Did the epidemic mainly involve American writers?*

There is very little systematic evidence available. In 1906 a questionnaire was sent to 150 German poets and writers, asking whether they drank alcohol before writing. Of the 115 writers who responded, seven drank in order to help their work, although twelve described its beneficial effects upon fantasy. A similar study was attempted in Sweden but most writers refused to cooperate.

In the introduction I counted forty-eight well-known American writers who gained a reputation for alcoholism more or less in the first half of the twentieth century. The same thirty-minute poll can be conducted with non-American writers.

Limiting the list to the dead, one comes up with twenty-eight probable alcoholics from six countries covering two centuries: Robert Burns, Algernon Swinburne, Lionel Johnson, Malcolm Lowry, Ernest Dowson, Paul Verlaine, Dylan Thomas, Brendan Behan, Evelyn Waugh, Sergei Yesenin, W.H. Auden, James Boswell, Samuel Johnson, Albert Camus, G.K. Chesterton, Samuel Coleridge, Ernst Hoffman, James Joyce, Alfred de Musset, Guy de Maupassant, Flann O'Brien, Arthur Rimbaud, Charles Baudelaire, Jean Rhys, Friedrich von Schiller, Oscar Wilde, Louis Mac-Neice, and Itzik Manger (the only Jewish writer on the list). Fourteen wrote in the twentieth century. Doubtless there were more, but it is unlikely that any other country ever had such a high proportion of alcoholic writers as America produced in roughly half a century.

There was much drinking by college boys at Cambridge and Oxford after World War I, as there was much beer drinking at the German universities. The literary pub life in England was a thriving industry in the years after World War II. America surely set a record.

In these comparisons, a question is often raised about reliability. Can you believe writers who say they don't drink much? Major symptoms of alcoholism, after all, are denial and rationalization—psychiatric jargon for lying. Maybe German and English writers lie about their drinking more than American writers.

A poll conducted by *Writer's Digest* bears on the point. Some years ago the *Digest* sent a questionnaire about drinking to well-known

American writers. Forty responded. (E.B. White said he was too busy drinking and writing to respond.)

Of the forty, only three confessed to an alcohol problem. John Ciardi said that he put away a fifth a night to help him sleep. One said he used to drink a lot but had switched to pot. A third described his drinking habits as "legendary." Some hedged. Norman Mailer described himself as a "medium" drinker. Maybe he is today, but he once told a *Time* interviewer that half his brain had been destroyed by alcohol. Comments Barnaby Conrad: "Norman Mailer, who has been known to do some bizarre and almost lethal things while under the influence, modestly describes his drinking as 'medium': that appears to be an understatement ranking with Alexander Woollcott's describing Lizzie Borden as 'unfilial.' "

One writer preferred to answer the questionnaire in the pages of the *New Yorker.* On learning that the *Writer's Digest* was planning a cover story on writing and drinking and wanted to include him, his "scandalized" response was: *"How did they find out?* I mean, I do take a drink now and again. In fact my doctor, who is the soul of tact, once characterized my consumption as 'slightly imprudent.' But how the devil did *Writer's Digest* discover this? Does the *whole city* know?"

The *New Yorker,* by the way, publishes about twenty cartoons a week. Based on a year's sample, one-quarter of the cartoons show a person holding an alcoholic beverage. One-sixth show a person drunk. The editors obviously find drinking humorous. So do many Americans. For the eight writers in this book, the humorous aspects of drinking, toward the end, probably escaped them.

For epidemiological purposes, the *Writer's Digest* poll is not very helpful. A certain evasiveness seems obvious, often cloaked in humor. Why do Americans find alcoholism so funny? Humor, to use a Freudian term, is a defense mechanism often invoked to mask anger. Why are the writers angry?

When suspecting alcoholism in a patient, a physician sometimes administers the CAGE test. It consists of four questions:

Have you ever:
* felt the need to Cut down on drinking?
* felt Annoyed by criticism of your drinking?
* had Guilty feelings about drinking
* taken a morning Eye-opener?

Patients who say yes to all four are usually alcoholic. The responders to the poll were clearly annoyed. This suggests that they were at least *one-quarter* alcoholic! It is interesting that jokes about drinking are more common in the United States than elsewhere. When American writers respond to drinking questions with humor and annoyance, it suggests Americans, in their way, may lie about drinking *at least* as much as other people. This may or may not settle the "reliability" issue but the epidemic, until proven otherwise, remains a largely American phenomenon.

2. *Did the epidemic chiefly occur in the first half of the twentieth century? What is happening in the second half?*
Except for Poe, it's hard to think of an alcoholic writer in America during the eighteenth and nineteenth centuries. Bret Harte, perhaps. Mark Twain liked to drink and there is a story about how he and Artemous Ward had crawled over the rooftops of Virginia City after a wild all-night party. He seemed ashamed of drinking. In the 1860s he wrote a friend that he got drunk only once every three months: "It sets a man back in the esteem of people whose opinions are worth having." He said he loved to drink, but didn't encourage drunkenness by "harping on its funny side." He was once jailed for being drunk. A biographer writes:

> At one time his drinking got all mixed up with his health fads, and he got it into his head that he needed hot Scotch or champagne or ale or beer—the formula varied from time to time—to put him to sleep. In a letter written for publication in 1883, he disclaimed being an expert on the effects of alcohol on thinking and writing, but he did say that, though he found two glasses of champagne "the happiest inspiration for an after-dinner speech," he felt wine "a clog to the pen, not an inspiration," and could not write after drinking even one glass.

Twain was not an alcoholic.
The long list of American writers who were alcoholic consists largely of writers who produced most of their work in the first half of the twentieth century. Tennessee Williams, John Cheever, and Truman Capote, together with some others, continued writing well

into the second half of the century, but their reputations were established in the 1940s.

The epidemic may have cooled off in the second half. There may be as many alcoholic writers, but they are not as visible. Most of the writers who got started in the 1950s are still living—too early for biographers. There are a few millionaire writers but most produce potboilers. There seem now to be fewer well-known writers than thirty or forty years ago. Certainly fewer are lionized. Television has claimed many and probably has the same sapping effect on talent as movies had earlier. A few contemporary writers—Elmore Leonard, James Dickey, Jill Robinson, Raymond Carver, Lawrence Block—talk frankly about having had a drinking problem but they represent a small minority of working writers. Shortly before he died in 1984, Truman Capote said that every writer he knew was alcoholic, but his judgment may have been distorted by his own serious drinking problem.

Something else happened in the last half of the century: a drug epidemic. The victims included rock and movie stars. They drank, but drugs were their downfall: heroin, cocaine, speed, and the new "designer" drugs synthesized by amateur chemists working in home basements. The casualties included Jimi Hendrix, Jim Morrison, Janis Joplin, Judy Garland, Marilyn Monroe, and John Belushi. They all died of drug overdose (although to the list of drugs must be added older ones such as barbiturates and tranquilizers). Undoubtedly only a small minority of those addicted to drugs died of them. Some, like John Lennon, often showed paranoid symptoms. Others checked into the Betty Ford Clinic, often the occasion for a press conference. Others became perpetual burdens to their families and society.

Drinking writers seemed for a time to be forgotten. *Newsweek* did a cover story on the great crime writer Elmore Leonard, and talked some of how he wrote better now that he had joined AA, but generally the topic was ignored.

Maybe drinking writers *are* a diminishing breed. If they don't talk about it and nobody writes about them, who can say? In any case, few people in the 1970s and 80s were asked the question posed by Sinclair Lewis in the 1950s: "Can you name five American writers since Poe who did *not* die of alcoholism?" In the first half of the century nobody doubted who died of what, and it wasn't of drugs (unless alcohol is considered a drug, which it is).

Before going on to the next topic, a question should be raised: Why the change? Was alcohol, for example, more available in the first half of the century and drugs in the second? Had attitudes changed toward drinking? Alcohol was equally available in both halves. Until the Harrison law of 1914, drugs were massively available. Opiates, marijuana-containing products, chloral hydrate, and nostrums galore could be bought at the drugstore without a prescription. Millions bought them and millions were hooked. Nobody knows how many because nobody took a poll. The Sears Roebuck catalog of 1901 had as many pages on drugs for morphine addiction as pages on the treatment of alcoholism, suggesting one may have been as prevalent as the other.

After 1914, drugs were less available in the United States, but nearly everyone could obtain chloral hydrate and paraldehyde, both addictive. Cocaine was both popular and available in the jazz age, although Cole Porter, for one, "got no kick from cocaine." Nevertheless, until the 1960s and the flower children, alcohol was overwhelmingly the drug of choice among Americans. Did the newly available street drugs reduce the use of alcohol? The answer is no. Alcohol sales continued to rise from 1950 to 1980, decreasing slightly in the 80s. (People also were using slightly less marijuana in the 80s.) Attitudes toward alcohol had changed: being legal, drinking was perhaps slightly less fun.

Availability may explain partly the shift to drugs, but probably not all. As for writers, there may not have been a shift. A case will be made later in this chapter that alcoholics are loners and that alcohol is a loner's drug. Stimulants like amphetamines and cocaine give fast highs that help rock stars (as well as athletes and actors) get "up" for a performance, and the effect is no doubt amplified if the audience is up also. Writing requires a sustained effort: highs don't help.

So, to the question "Are writers drinking less?" the answer is *probably.* To the question "Is the drinking writer the celebrity he once was?" the answer is a categorical *no.*

3. *Did the epidemic also involve creative people in the other arts?*
Probably, to some extent. One can draw up a fairly impressive list of Hollywood stars who were alcoholic or at least had the reputation of being one (for example, W.C. Fields, Buster Keaton, Bing Crosby,

John Barrymore, Humphrey Bogart, Spencer Tracy, Ava Gardner), and numerous directors and others in the movie business had alcohol problems. No list of Hollywood stars, however, probably would include more than 10 percent considered alcoholic.

Another susceptible group was jazz musicians. Few classical performers had a drinking problem, one reason being that the technical demands of fingering a violin, say, are such that one can't have two or three drinks and do it. Roger Kahn detects influences of alcohol in English music dating back to the Elizabethans, but reliable biographical information about musicians of earlier periods is too skimpy to make judgments.

It is said that painters are heavy drinkers. Again, no data exist. The closest thing we have is a study by Anne Roe in the 1940s. She interviewed twenty eminent painters and found that all drank, but none seemed alcoholic.

4. *Did the epidemic mainly involve well-known writers?*

When I raised this question in a journal article, I received a letter from a reader in public relations, writing: "Let me state firmly that alcoholism does affect the unrecognized and/or mediocre writer. I know. I am both."

This is the only "hard data" I have on the subject, other than stories about heavy-drinking newspapermen, few famous. In the *Writer's Digest* survey, John Jakes said the hardest drinkers he had met were copywriters in the advertising business. Are one-third of advertising copywriters alcoholic? No studies have been done.

No doubt some writers are better known for their drinking than for their writing, especially "difficult" poets like Dylan Thomas and John Berryman. Many who have never read a line by either poet know the reputation of each for drinking. Berryman was a minor poet with a microscopic audience until he made the cover of *Life* with a reporter following him on a pub crawl. The caricaturist David Levine pictured Berryman with an enormous bottle down his back. After he became a celebrity, perhaps more people read him, but not many. He became permanently enshrined in the mythology of the tragic writer-alcoholic when he committed suicide by jumping from a bridge in Minneapolis onto the frozen Mississippi River.

There are other examples of writers who apparently become

celebrities from their boozing more than from their large readership. "I suppose hundreds of people in three decades have seen Sinclair Lewis drunk, no doubt he made a vast public spectacle of himself," wrote his former secretary, Barnaby Conrad, and the same can be said of Fitzgerald, Thomas Wolfe, and others. They all made spectacles of themselves. Scott and his wife would do things like "riding on the tops of taxicaps, flooding hotel rooms by leaving the bathroom tap on, or bathing in the Plaza's fountain nude at midnight, or making an omelet in a stranger's derby in a restaurant, ad nauseam, ad delirium tremens, ad mortis" (a memorable line by Conrad). One night, when Fitzgerald and Wolfe were arguing, Wolfe gesticulated so strenuously that he struck a powerline support, snapped the wire, and plunged the whole community into darkness. Wolfe was six feet nine. He died in 1938 of tuberculosis of the brain, but, according to Conrad, "the Brobdingnagian body had been the brunt of terrible alcoholic assaults and insults since college days. It is astonishing that so much literary output was produced in, and around, so much alcohol." Lewis had a big readership but was not a very good writer; Wolfe had small audiences but was a genius; Fitzgerald was read widely at first but by few at the end. The drinking was an indispensable element of their fame; the media made sure of it.

To answer the question: It is impossible to know whether obscure writers are as frequently alcoholic as well-known writers, for the obvious reason that well-known writers are well known and obscure writers are obscure.

5. *Did the epidemic involve specifically alcohol, or were other drugs also abused?*

Opium and opium products were widely used and sometimes abused by writers and poets in nineteenth-century England. Laudanum—tincture of opium—was freely available and used by nice little ladies there. The drug was available in the United States but, with the possible exception of Poe, was rarely used by American writers (or they didn't talk about it).

Cannabis products, particularly hashish, were used by French symbolists in Baudelaire's nineteenth-century France but, like opium, came under regulation in the twentieth century and their role in literary life was reduced.

Twentieth-century American writers have used other drugs than alcohol. The eight writers discussed in this book all used barbiturates or other sedatives, usually to help them stay sober or overcome insomnia. A minority—Dorothy Parker, Tennessee Williams, and Truman Capote come to mind—apparently abused barbiturates and tranquilizers as much as alcohol. For most alcoholic writers in the twentieth century's first half, alcohol was the "drug of choice."

Whether this is changing in the second half is not really known. In the *Writer's Digest* survey four writers suggest that alcohol may be taking a back seat to marijuana, amphetamines, and cocaine, but they had no evidence for this. Stephen King says that he never wrote anything "worth a dime" under the influence of pot or hallucinogens and considers alcohol an "extremely benign poison." The late Thomas Thompson said that marijuana was better than alcohol in curing writer's block. Michael Crichton says he knows many writers who take amphetamines when they work and affirm their usefulness. Crichton disagrees with the practice. Amphetamines, Ritalin, or massive doses of coffee are "exactly the wrong substance to take, since they tend to make you obsess on some subject and not loosen up, and tend to increase paranoia." Crichton subscribes to the "orality" theory of the writer-alcohol connection: for those writers who take pills or have a drink it's the *fact* of taking the pill or drink that is important, not the ingested substance.

As suggested earlier, this may not be true. Alcohol has special pharmacological properties suited to a writer's needs. It provokes fantasy (as do other drugs) but also promotes sociability (other drugs usually don't). It can be consumed over long periods, "titrated" to achieve a delicate balance between drunkenness and serenity (a balance few drinkers can sustain for long). Writers can write and drink simultaneously (although most wish they hadn't) but this is less true with other drugs (who wants to plot novels during a cocaine high?). Finally, there is a point made already and the subject of much to come: writers are loners and alcoholism is a loner's disease.

An epidemic of alcoholism among American writers in the first half of the twentieth century appears to have occurred. The epidemic apparently involved alcohol more than other drugs. Whether the epidemic mainly involved well-known writers cannot be answered, but fame plus alcohol made writers do many silly things and their well-knownness may trace as much to this as to their writing. Maybe the connection is between exhibitionism and writing rather than drinking and writing, but it seems unlikely.

Accepting these propositions, we ask, What caused the epidemic?

Causes

For something so often talked about, the drinking-writer connection has hardly been studied at all. There has been a book or two on the subject, plus a few articles; that's all.

Most of the writers polled by the *Writer's Digest*, when asked whether they thought drinking and writing had common roots, shrugged and said, "Who knows?" Michael Crichton, who took the question seriously, pointed out that different people may be drawn to the same things for different reasons, and that for one person the meaning of a dependence may change with time.

"That is," he said, "I don't think necessarily that Hemingway and Malcolm Lowry drank for the same reasons—and I don't think that Hemingway's drinking patterns as a young man had the same significance to him as his drinking patterns later in life."

Alfred Kazin made the same point: "People drink for hereditary reasons, nutritional reasons, social reasons. They drink because they are bored, or tired, or restless. People drink for as many reasons as they have for wanting to 'feel better.'"

In short, the problem may be unstudiable. There will always be theoretically minded people who will cram the writer-drinker phenomenon into a favorite theory, but the connection seems to resist the scientific method. Perhaps, as Sir Arthur Eddington said, "All our knowledge is ultimately derived from pointer readings" (temperature gauges, wristwatches, etc.) and no pointers explain the drinking writer.

Still, curiosity is not satisfied by saying many writers drank, and isn't that interesting. The rest of this chapter gives reasons why writers may drink more than plumbers or even movie actors, and concludes with some thoughts about why American writers were the main victims of the recent epidemic.

1. *The hours are good*

Several years ago the National Council on Alcoholism had a forum in which four authors discussed drinking and writing (the four had considerable experience with both). Much attention was paid to the fact that writers don't punch a time clock.

Ring Lardner, Jr., suggested that they drink heavily because writing is an occupation that doesn't require specific hours. "It's much easier for [alcoholism] to become deeply rooted when you can go for several days without working and you can fix your own time." Roger Kahn pointed out that maybe that's one reason people become writers: nobody checks on them. "Unlike a psychiatrist," he said, "nobody comes in every hour to see you." He felt psychiatrists led unhealthful lives but they were still better off than those who went into a room and thought up conversations that never happened.

Continuing, Kahn said that "nobody knows the skills the drinking writers use to produce a certain amount of work. By the time the spouse or somebody else arrives, he can be moderately drunk and [have] brushed his teeth, but little work is done, and nobody knows. That's probably unique to the writer. Somebody will know in eighteen months when you don't have the book, or in five years when you don't have a career.

"It's the privacy that distinguishes the writer. The ability to drink from nine in the morning until five at night" while pretending to work.

Lardner chimed in: "If you feel too weak or your head is aching too much to function at the typewriter, you can say to your wife and children, you're thinking, and make it look as if you are thinking and you create an illusion, and you might spend a whole day at it without getting out a line." Even drinking might be forgiven for a time: "You must understand the kind of pressure I am under because I am creating" is the usually unspoken motto of the drinking writer.

It cannot be assumed that a particular job causes a drinking problem. Bartenders have the highest alcoholism rate, not necessarily because they are bartenders but maybe because some bartenders become bartenders because of the proximity of booze. Postmen have the lowest rate—that is, the lowest cirrhosis rate. The mailcarrier has to be up at dawn and trudge for miles (at least in the old days), carrying a seventy-five-pound bag on his back. If he misses too much work, his pay is docked. Delivering mail from door to door in all kinds of weather is not exactly the job a man would choose who is likely to have a hangover.

People choose jobs and jobs choose people.

There also was a good deal of talk about the loneliness of creative writing. Jill Robinson expressed the opinion that one finds in writers and alcoholics similar personality traits. "There is a paradoxical allure and fear of loneliness, the remoteness, the urgency to express feeling in whatever possible way, and to remove oneself from it as soon as it is recognized. I strongly maintain alcoholism comes *before* writing—lurks there in the frequently talented child."

Others don't find the act of writing lonely at all. They become lost in the creative act and have as many companions as they wish, simply by inventing them.

2. *It is expected*

People *do* what is expected of them. In early twentieth-century America, writers and poets were expected to be tragic, lonely, and doomed. Excessive drinking is a manifestation of this image. It is a manifestation that meets the expectations of oneself and of society.

Poe introduced the romantic tradition to American literature. It was compounded of one part Byron, one part Mary Shelley, one part Baudelaire, and one part early southern Gothic. Passionate love, dissipation, and early death were all part of the tradition. Baudelaire believed intoxication was essential to creativity, and the source of the intoxication was irrelevant:

> One must always be intoxicated. That's the main thing: it's the only issue. In order to feel the horrible burden of Time which breaks your shoulders and bows you to the earth, you must become intoxicated without respite. But with what? With wine, with poetry or with virtue, as you please.

Nietzsche, a German romantic, agreed. In *Twilight of the Idols* he writes: "For art to exist, for any sort of aesthetic activity to exist, a certain physiological precondition is indispensable: intoxication." Any intoxicant would do: sex, the weather, narcotics. "In this condition [intoxication] one enriches everything out of one's own abundance; what one sees, what one desires, one sees swollen, pressing, strong, overladen with energy."

Fifty years after Poe died a second wide-eyed romantic came onto the American literary scene: Jack London. Like Poe, he found intoxication readily available in a bottle. He wrote a remarkable book called *John Barleycorn* about his alcoholism. Shortly before his death at forty from an overdose of morphine (Poe also died at forty), London tells what the bottle really contained:

> John Barleycorn *makes* toward death . . . it is a terrible ordeal for a man to stand upright on his two legs unswaying, and decide that in all the universe he finds for himself but one freedom— namely, the anticipating of the day of his death. With this man this is the hour of the white logic. . . . Of course, all this is soul- sickness, life-sickness. It is the penalty the imaginative man must pay for his friendship with John Barleycorn. . . . to the imagina- tive man, John Barleycorn sends the pitiless spectral syllogisms of the white logic. . . . He sees; he knows. And he knows his one freedom: he may anticipate the day of his death. . . . Alcohol tells truth, but its truth is not normal. . . . John Barleycorn [comes] with the curse he lays upon the imaginative man who is lusty with life and desire to live. John Barleycorn sends his White Logic, the argent messenger of truth beyond truth, the antithesis of life, cruel and bleak as interstellar space, pulseless and frozen as abso- lute zero, dazzling with the frost of irrefragable logic and unforgettable fact.

London died in 1916. After him the epidemic developed with tidal force. Writers were expected to live in the romantic tradition and many strove mightily to fulfill the expectation.

"If you are an artist," John Cheever wrote, "self-destruction is quite expected of you. The thrill of staring into the abyss is exciting until it becomes, as it did in my case, contemptible." At one low point Cheever was almost jailed for drunkenness:

> There was this bum drinking out of a brown paper bag so I sat down with him. This was precisely what my parents would not

have wanted me to do. We both drank out of the brown paper bag—it was some kind of fortified wine—and a policeman came along and threatened to arrest us.

In the twentieth century, society came to expect drunkenness in its famous writers. According to Leslie Fiedler, every age required that its geniuses have a fatal "charismatic" flaw: blindness in the Homeric age, incest in Byron's time, homosexuality in the *fin de siècle,* and in twentieth-century America preeminently drunkenness.

For all the talk about how boring drunks are, they can also have a fatal fascination. Albert Finney, "drunk" throughout the movie *Under the Volcano,* maintained the otherworldly dignity of the alcoholic who has "drunk himself sober." Apparently Ring Lardner often looked that way. In *Tender Is the Night* Fitzgerald modeled his character Abe after his former neighbor Lardner:

Resignedly Abe shook hands with Rosemary; he composed his face slowly, holding her hand a long time and forming sentences that did not emerge. She laughed in a well-bred way, as though it were nothing unusual to watch a man walking in a slow dream. Often people display a curious respect for a man drunk, rather like the respect of simple races for the insane. Respect rather than fear. There is something awe-inspiring in one who has lost all inhibitions, who will do anything. Of course we make him pay for his moment of superiority, his moment of impressiveness.

The moral is this: societies, like individuals, get the sorts of drunken comportment that they allow. A book called *Drunken Comportment* makes the point forcefully in the following anecdote, which dates from the England of the early 1660s:

The story goes that not long after James I acceded to the throne, a certain English nobleman gave a dinner party to which he invited a large number of luminaries. After the goblets had been filled and refilled several times and the liquor had taken hold, an English general named Somerset rose from his chair and proclaimed: "Gentlemen, when I am in my cups, and the generous wine begins to warm my blood, I have an absurd custom of railing against the Scottish people. Knowing my weakness, I hope no gentlemen in the company will take it amiss."

Having thus delivered himself, he sat down, and a Highland

chief, one Sir Robert Blackie of Blair-Antholl, rose and with sin-
gular dispassion addressed his fellow celebrants as follows:

"Gentlemen, when I am in *my* cups, and the generous wine
begins to warm my blood, if I hear a man rail against the Scottish
people, I have an absurd custom of kicking him at once out of the
company, often breaking a few of his bones in the process. Knowing my weakness, I hope no gentlemen will take it amiss."

The story concludes, we need scarcely add, that General Somerset did not that night follow his usual custom of denigrating the
Scottish people.

By the 1970s the stereotype of the drunken writer had become so
established in America that a Boston-Irish short story writer named
Ralph Maloney could view his disease as a job like any other and at
the same time invest it with the romantic despair that is the hallmark
of the tradition:

Every stance is a posture, every face a pose. We are all victims
of mirrors and mother's hope. There is no purpose in it all, no
master plan. Alcoholism, like accountancy or medicine, is only
somebody to be, as are the priesthood, the military and the law.
When it is over, the dark diceman comes to visit us all. Death is at
the end of every street, no matter how you hedge or scramble,
and the greatest effort and the least effort are equally rewarded
with gravel in the face. You won't be back, don't kid yourself.
Neither will I. The world will be just as keen or ugly without us.
So, in the pretty girl's sweet, deliberate wink that we're here, let
us be somebody we like. Work for pleasure. Marry a friend.

Maloney died at forty.

3. *Writers need inspiration*

One reason writers have trouble writing is what Simenon calls
"stage fright": they are not sure they can do it, or do it well anyway.

Like baseball players who bat .300 one week and go hitless the
next, writers are at the mercy of something beyond their control.
The batter's reputation, his income, and professional future depend
entirely on reflexes over which he has little influence; the writer's
depend on something called inspiration, which is just as capricious.
Some days you hit the ball, others you don't. This is why early success for some writers has been disastrous. How can you do it *again*
when you have no idea how you did it before?

(This may explain why baseball players seem also to have a fairly high rate of alcoholism. John Lardner described one ballplayer as a righthanded hitter but a switch drinker: "He could raise a glass with either hand." Babe Ruth, the greatest of the alcoholic ballplayers, died early. The funeral took place on a hot day and went on and on. Walking outdoors afterward, one Yankee said, "Christ, I would give my right arm for a cold beer," and the other said, "So would the Babe.")

There are three opinions about whether alcohol provides inspiration for writers. One holds that it never does, another that it sometimes does, and a third that it is essential.

According to the first view, drinking writers create their own masterpieces not *on account of* alcohol, but *in spite of* it. Still, Fitzgerald and Simenon (among others) believed they had to drink to write. (Fitzgerald said that his "creative vitality demanded stimulation.")

Rather large numbers of drinking writers believe alcohol helps *sometimes.* "Drink heightens feeling," Fitzgerald told a friend. "When I drink, it heightens my emotions and I put it in a story. . . . My stories written when sober are stupid . . . all reasoned out, not felt." "A writer who drinks carefully is probably a better writer," says Stephen King. "The main effect of the grain or the grape on the creative personality is that it provides the necessary sense of newness and freshness, without which creative writing does not occur." The reasoning goes like this:

As a child the writer could spend hours alone in his fantasy world, but as an adult he may find he has lost the knack. A reverie may be an escape, but it is also necessary for his work, and alcohol makes it easier. Cheever noted that growing older is accompanied by dulling of the senses: "subtle distance comes between you and the smell of wood smoke." Alcohol permits the writer to see things freshly. Its toxic effect on the brain can restore the sense of wonder at the world that children experience, that is essential to the motivation to write.

Drinking *does* produce a kind of chemical trance, an "altered state of consciousness" in the current jargon. If alcohol really does help writers write, this may be why. "Genius," William James said, "is little more than the faculty of perceiving in an unhabitual way." Nongeniuses, intoxicated, see the world in an unhabitual way.

Alcohol does make events and ideas seem meaningful and important. "At times," Arnold Ludwig writes, speaking of trance states in general, "it appears as though the person is undergoing an attenuated 'eureka' experience, during which feelings of profound insight, illumination, and truth frequently occur." Ludwig concedes this "sense of increased significance" may bear little relationship to truth. But for writers this is not the point. They *must* view people and events and ideas as significant. Otherwise, why experience all that pain to write about them? Angus Wilson says he has to persuade himself of the "truth" of what he writes about before he can persuade his readers. And one of the "charms of drunkenness," as William James said, "unquestionably lies in the deepening sense of reality and truth which is gained therein. In whatever light things may then appear to us, they seem more utterly what they are, more 'utterly utter' than when we are sober."

In *Under the Volcano*, the consul, drunk after a day and a night of imbibing, told his wife that "unless you drink as I do, can you hope to understand the beauty of an old woman from Tarasco who plays dominoes at seven o'clock in the morning? All mystery, all hope, all disappointment, yes, all disaster, is here, beyond those swinging doors"—for the drinker. Art Hill comments: "This capacity to invest the ordinary or the ugly with an aura of beauty—very real, however fleeting—is the one positive justification ever put forward for the alcoholic's addiction. All other reasons are defensive, mere excuses."

On this basis drinking writers sometimes deride nondrinking writers. Norman Douglas, in *South Wind*, asks: "Have you ever heard of a teetotaler conspicuous for kindliness of heart, or intellectually distinguished in any walk of life? I should be glad to know his name. A sorry crew! Not because they drink water, but because the state of mind which makes them dread alcohol is unpropitious to the hatching of any generous idea." Even Bernard Shaw, a teetotaler, acknowledged the mythical potency of drink. "Not everybody," he wrote, "is strong enough to endure life without an anesthetic" and conceded that "drink probably averts more gross crime than it causes."

Nevertheless, writers who have relied solely on alcohol for inspiration have lived to regret it. Simenon found he could write just as well or better without alcohol. Fitzgerald always regretted writing the second half of *Tender Is the Night* while drinking. He said a short story could be written on a bottle, but "for a novel you need the mental speed that enables you to keep the whole pattern in your head." His last uncompleted work, written sober, might have been his best.

Moreover, alcohol-induced revelations often can't be trusted. The same is true of chemical-induced revelations in general. Oliver Wendell Holmes sniffed ether and reported of the universe: "The whole is pervaded with the smell of turpentine." William James tried nitrous oxide, wrote down a cosmic discovery, and found the next day that the cosmic discovery was "higamous, hogamus, woman's monogamous, hogamus, higamus, man is polygamous." After LSD, a psychologist received the ultimate secret of the universe: "Please flush after using."

The next morning, after scribbling feverishly on bar napkins, the writer is often faced with unintelligible drivel.

Except for providing inspiration, does alcohol otherwise help writers write? If it does—a big if—here are two ways it might do so.

It may help in starting and help in stopping.

For most writers, the hardest thing about writing is getting started. Many rely on ritual. Hemingway sharpened twenty pencils. Willa Cather read a passage from the Bible. Thomas Wolfe roamed the streets. Another novelist, an agnostic, got down on his knees and started the working day with a prayer.

Others drink. A.E. Housman was an example. "Having drunk a pint of beer at luncheon," he wrote, "I would go out for a walk. As I went along, there would flow into my mind, with sudden and unaccountable emotion, sometimes a line or two of verse, sometimes a whole stanza. . . ."

"Before I start to write, I always treat myself to a nice dry martini," says E.B. White, "Just one, to give me the courage to get started. After that, I am on my own."

Writers need courage. "In a writer," Tolstoy wrote, "there must always be two people—the *writer* and the *critic*." Alcohol silences the critic.

Ironically, once the creative process gets under way, writers often have trouble stopping it, and alcohol may serve a need here too. It happened with Truman Capote. Interviewed, he said that once he began writing

> in fearful earnest, my mind zoomed all night every night, and I don't think I really slept for several years. Not until I discovered that whisky could relax me. I was too young, fifteen, to buy it myself, but I had a few older friends who were most obliging in this respect and I soon accumulated a suitcase full of bottles, everything from blackberry brandy to bourbon. I kept the suitcase hidden in a closet. Most of my drinking was done in the late afternoon; then I'd chew a handful of Sen Sen and go down to dinner, where my behavior, my glazed silences, gradually grew into a source of general consternation. One of my relatives used to say, "Really, if I didn't know better, I'd swear he was dead drunk."

James Thurber also found a drink helped terminate writing. It often needed terminating. Sometimes his wife would come up to him at a dinner party and say, "Damn it, Thurber, stop writing." "She usually catches me in the middle of a paragraph," Thurber commented. Once his daughter looked up from the dinner table and asked, "Is he sick?" "No," said Thurber's wife, "he's writing."

Thurber was a compulsive as well as an obsessional writer. He rewrote and rewrote. He said of one story that there must have been two hundred forty thousand words in all the manuscripts put together and he spent two thousand hours working at it. Yet the finished story was less than two thousand words.

There is a third way alcohol may facilitate creative thinking. Some people believe they write best when feeling poorly. T.S. Eliot said he wrote best when anemic. Turgenev said he could write only when painfully in love: "Now I am old and I can't fall in love any more, and that is why I have stopped writing."

With Freud it was bowels. His best work came after a bout with an irritable colon. "I can't be industrious when I am in good health," he wrote.

Perhaps a little hangover helps the Muse along.

Writing, in any case, is hard work. In Anthony Burgess's words, it is "excruciating to the body: it engenders tobacco addiction, an over-reliance on caffeine and Dexedrine, piles, dyspepsia, chronic anxiety, sexual impotence." How he overlooked alcohol addiction is a mystery.

Simenon recommends that no one write unless he has to.

> I think that anyone who does not *need* to be a writer, who thinks he can do something else, ought to do something else. Writing is not a profession but a vocation of unhappiness. I don't think an artist can ever be happy.

So why do writers write? "Because," Simenon said, "I think that if a man has the urge to be an artist, it is because he needs to find himself. Every writer tries to find himself through his characters."

The Loner Theory

Who is this "self" writers seek? Are writers different from other people? Are their selves harder to find? Does alcohol aid in the search?

Historian Gilman Ostrander has an interesting theory about this. Here are excerpts from a letter that Dr. Ostrander wrote about his theory:

> Alcoholism is basically a disease of individualism. It afflicts people who from early childhood develop a strong sense of being psychologically alone and on their own in the world. This solitary outlook prevents them from gaining emotional release through associations with other people, but they find they can get this emotional release by drinking. So they become dependent on alcohol in the way other people are dependent on their social relationships with friends and relatives.

Writers, Ostrander believes, are also loners and this is one reason they write. "It is a profession which allows the individual to be tremendously convivial all by himself. . . . Writing and drinking are two forms of companionship."

Ostrander also believes his theory explains why alcoholism is more prevalent in some ethnic groups than in others. The high alcoholism rate among the Irish and French, he says, is at least partly traceable to the fact that Irish and French children are brought up to be "responsible for their own conduct. When they grow up and leave the household, they are expected to be able to take care of themselves. Individualism in this sense is highly characteristic of these groups."

Jews and Japanese, on the other hand, have a low alcoholism rate, and this is because children are *not* expected to be independent.

> Infants in these families are badly spoiled, that is to say, their whims are indulged in by parents and older relatives, so that, from the outset, they become emotionally dependent upon others in the family. . . . It is never possible for them to acquire the sense of separate identity, apart from their family, that is beaten into children in, say, Ireland. . . . They are likely to remain emotionally dependent upon and a part of their family in a way that is not true in societies where the coddling of children is socially disapproved of.

And this is why Ostrander believes most Jews and even hard-drinking Japanese do not become alcoholic. "They never had the chance to think of themselves as individuals in the Western sense of the word. They are brought up to be so dependent upon others in the family that they are unable to think of themselves as isolated individuals." They do not need alcohol to give them a "sense of emotional completeness."

It is a hard theory to prove. Still, whether most alcoholics are loners or not, most creative writers are, or believe they are. In the biographies of famous writers, no theme recurs so frequently as loneliness, shyness, isolation. Simenon, for example, has declared that he is haunted by the problem of communication.

> I mean communication between two people. The fact that we are I don't know how many millions of people, yet communication, complete communication, is completely impossible between two of those people, is to me one of the biggest tragic themes in the world. When I was a young boy I was afraid of it. I would almost scream because of it. It gave me such a sensation of solitude, or loneliness.

This may be one reason writers write. They can communicate with their characters. It may also be one reason they *can* write. Distance gives perspective. It may further—if Ostrander is right—be one reason they drink.

Both writing and drinking bear certain similarities to trance states. Psychiatrist Arnold Ludwig observes that trances "tend to lessen the differentiation between self and others and therefore . . . [promote] greater social cohesiveness. . . ." When writing, Simenon is almost literally in a trance. He sees nobody, speaks to nobody. "I live just like a monk. All the day I am one of my characters. I feel what he feels." For eleven days—he writes a chapter a day—he is in the "character's skin." This is one reason his novels are so short. After eleven days he is utterly exhausted. And after he finishes a novel he can never remember what it was about. (If you talk to him about one of his books, he gives you a blank stare, as if hearing about it for the first time.) Trances, Ludwig says, often end with amnesia; so, at least for Simenon, does novel writing.

Faulkner also used to stare at people when they asked about something he wrote. "Hell, how do I know what it means? I was drunk when I wrote it."

The loner theory explains much. For example:

1. Writing and alcohol both produce trancelike states. A gift for creative writing may involve an innate ability to enter trancelike states. Being a loner—shy, isolated, without strong personal ties—may facilitate trancelike states when it is time to write and encourage drinking to overcome the shyness and isolation when it is time to relax.

2. Creative writing requires a rich fantasy life; loners have rich fantasy lives—the ultimate loner is the schizophrenic who lives in a prison of fantasy. Alcohol promotes fantasy.

3. People with so-called multiple personalities are said to be loners regardless of the personality they assume. The writers in this book can all be said to have multiple personalities: they were chameleons, always changing, particularly when drunk. Invariably shy—even Hemingway—they become gregarious when drunk, often behaved like fools, were often mean.

Scotty Fitzgerald described her father as a "totally different person when drunk: not just gay or tiddly, but *mean*." "After a few drinks," wrote Scott Donaldson, "Fitzgerald fastidiously blew his breath into his hands to see if it was offensive. After a few more, he went out of his way to offend."

Drunk or sober, they wore different masks for different occasions. Nobody could be nicer, or crueler than the writers in this book. (Ring Lardner, who is not in the book, apparently was an exception among alcoholic writers: he was always nice.)

Loners because they *couldn't* be close to people, they drank to become close, and then, when they became mean drunk, alcohol became their excuse the next day.

Drinking produced severe personality changes, or perhaps it wasn't a change, merely an intensification, as Stephen Longstreet described Hemingway: "He was a mean and cruel man, for all his vitality, audacity, and charm. His father had given him a shotgun at seven, and he was to spend a great deal of his life slaughtering thousands of birds, animals, big fish, and, in the end, the biggest game of all—himself."

John Cheever—going to AA meetings, trying to stay sober—wrote: "I write to make sense of my life." Writing made his life less chaotic, less depressing. When it worked, it did so barely: "That bridge of language, metaphors, anecdote and imagination that I build each morning to cross the incongruities in my life seems very frail indeed." For years alcohol had healed the incongruities, but it was killing him and writing was all he had left. "His loneliness," wrote his daughter Susan, "was so sharp that it sometimes felt like intestinal flu."

The creative person is a sensitive person. "You see," Truman Capote once said, "I was so different from everyone, so much more intelligent and sensitive and perceptive. I was having fifty perceptions a minute to everyone else's five. I always felt that nobody was going to understand me, going to understand what I felt about things. I guess that is why I started writing. At least on paper I could put down what I thought."

The writer and editor William McIlwain thought that was why writers drank: "A writer perhaps can't stand all the things he sees clearly and . . . must take the white glare out of the clarity."

Many writers complain of too much clarity. Lowry said he felt as if he had been born without a skin. Faulkner sometimes drank because of the exhaustion that came after the tension of writing: "I feel as though all my nerve ends were exposed."

I once received a letter from a self-styled obscure writer who said he felt the same way as Faulkner: "I doubt that you will find one writer who dips his pen into the emotions of other people's blood and tears, who, if honest, will not admit that after writing something frightening he is himself frightened, sometimes something sad may leave him sobbing over the keys of his typewriter, completely wrung out from the emotion that has been transmitted to paper." Continuing:

> This extreme sensitivity must have some effect on brain chemistry. The micro-electricity of the mind's synapses must move at a fearful pace as selections are made as rapidly as fingers can move over a typewriter or a quill scratch ink on foolscap. It is exhausting work. The brain is overcharged, running at full tilt. There is no "stop" button to turn off the circuitry. Alcohol pushes the "stop" button.
>
> I wonder what would happen if a study were made of the brain wave patterns of creative people at their work? Would the electroencephalogram show that the circuitry was pushing close to the point normally denoting mental disturbance? I think it would. Genius is close to insanity, if not in itself a form of insanity. . . . Which of the many little gray cell circuits must short out to place a person over the threshold and into the institution?

He concludes: "Since I stopped drinking, my creative ability has been diluted . . . a bottle of booze could, and did, turn it on."

Malcolm Lowry thought drinking prevented nervous breakdowns. The little-gray-circuit theory would have appealed to him.

Their storytelling gifts as children, their tortured sensitivity, their inability to mature completely, the incongruities in their personalities—all may reflect an inability to feel at home with people. With Thomas Wolfe and the rest, it wasn't just that they could not return home again; they didn't know where home was if they looked. John Cheever, shortly before his death, wrote: "The nature of [my] sorrow is bewildering. I seek some familiarity that eludes me. I want to go home and I have no home."

The psychological aloneness that seems to characterize these writers is something one also sees in clinical depressions. What can we say about the psychiatric status of the American alcoholic writers apart from their excessive drinking?

First, diagnosing a psychiatric illness in a person who is drinking heavily is impossible. Heavy drinking produces insomnia, depression, anxiety attacks, delusions, and hallucinations. Nevertheless, the writers in this book and most other alcoholic writers who lived long enough, did stop drinking for extended periods. Did they share common features when sober? Shyness and hypersensitivity, excessive individualism, are not technically psychiatric disorders.

Malcolm Cowley, who knew many of the alcoholic writers personally, thought many had manic-depressive disease. Depressed they all were, from time to time. Most had clinical depressions, but it was sometimes hard to tell whether alcohol was responsible. The euphoria and hyperactivity that characterize mania are not seen often in the biographies. Cheever, after he became sober in his sixties and found his writing talent intact, had "bursts of euphoria" that may have been mania but that also may have been mere expressions of the joy of being healthy. Robert Lowell is one of the few heavy-drinking writers who clearly had manic-depressive disease with definite periods of mania.

All had insomnia. All tried to cure it with alcohol and pills. All had it after they stopped drinking. If alcoholism is the writer's vice (Fitzgerald's phrase), insomnia is the writer's scourge.

All were hypochondriacs.

Most became paranoid when they drank and Hemingway was delusionally paranoid after he stopped drinking. Tennessee Williams thought people were putting ground glass into his vodka.

As a group they tended to be anxious people and some had clinical disorders called, variously, anxiety neurosis, generalized anxiety disorder, or severe social phobias. About one-third of alcoholics have anxiety disorders (which *may* have caused the alcoholism), and it is nouar whether alcoholic writers are more or less susceptible to these disabling states.

Some alcoholic writers were homosexual, but apparently not most.

Probably all could be described as having "oral" personalities, broadly defined. "Writers," Michael Crichton believes, "fall into that general category of people who relieve their anxiety by putting something in their mouths." The hard-drinking writer of the twenties and thirties, perhaps to some extent, has been replaced by multiple-drug-taking forms of behavior (according to Crichton) but it is still oral. Crichton says that he was well on his way to a "heavy drinking style" when he discovered that he was interested less in alcohol than in the act of swallowing. "I made the transition from compulsive booze-drinking to compulsive soft-drink drinking with little difficulty and I will now consume several quarts of Pepsi in a hard day at work."

Were any of the alcoholic writers nonsmokers? Yes, Hemingway. It is hard to think of others.

"Orality" is a behavior, not an explanation. Psychoanalysts, who often use the term, have contributed little to our understanding of the alcohol-writer connection. Freud wrote an essay on Dostoevski and concluded that his epilepsy was a manifestation of his hatred of his father (he had identified with his father and was now punishing himself by having fits), and Jung had some Olympian pronouncements on the subject, but otherwise, although free with terms like "orality" and "latent homosexuality," the psychoanalysts have had little to contribute.

Much of the above is based on impressions and anecdotes. There is a common idea, held by the ancient Greeks, amplified by Cesare Lombroso in the nineteenth century and by Edmund Wilson in the twentieth, that creativity and insanity are related—indeed arise from the same genes. Surprisingly, not a single study of scientific merit had documented this until late 1987—and this study had drawbacks, the main one being the small number of subjects (thirty).

Nancy Andreasen, a psychiatrist with a Ph.D. in English literature, conducted a study over a fifteen-year period, using for her subjects "creative writers" at the University of Iowa Writer's Workshop. (How creative? The writers are not identified, not even their ages.) Here is what she found. Compared to a control group of non-writers, matched for age, sex, education, and intelligence, the writers were

  a. more often depressed (37 percent)
  b. more often manic (43 percent)
  c. more often alcoholic (30 percent)

In all, twenty-four of the thirty writers had experienced depression or mania, or both—and two committed suicide during the fifteen-year study. (One wonders if John Berryman was one of the suicides; he was at Iowa during that period.) Moreover, these were not *impressions* of mental illness; these were *diagnoses* based on accepted medical criteria.

As noted, this is the first scientific study that ever showed a link between creativity and mental illness. No schizophrenia, by the way, was found in the group. Before the study, most authorities would probably have predicted that schizophrenia was more related to creativity than were depression and mania, but not so in this study.

Andreasen found something else interesting. Compared to control subjects, the creative writers had a high percentage of manic-depressive relatives and a high percentage of creative relatives. (Relatives were classified as creative people if they had a "well-recognized level of creative achievement, such as writing novels, dancing in a major company, performing as a concert artist or in a major symphony, or making a major scientific contribution such as an invention.")

Whereas 30 percent of the creative writers were alcoholic, only 7 percent of their relatives were alcoholic. This was surprising. Alcoholism generally runs in families. Not always, however. "Non-familial" alcoholics exist and they often have other psychiatric illnesses than alcoholism, one being manic-depressive disease. Is it possible the link between creativity and alcoholism is genetic (a "hereditary taint," as Lombroso said), but the genes connecting the two are actually the genes for manic-depressive illness and not the genes for alcoholism? (Studies indicate that both manic-depressive disease and alcoholism have a partial genetic basis.) This is a tantalizing possibility, consistent with many of the anecdotal accounts in this chapter ("I was having fifty perceptions a minute to every one else's five," wrote Truman Capote, and a less well-known writer said that his mind moved at a "fearful pace . . . the brain is over-charged, running at full tilt." This is precisely the way manics describe their thinking). And of course writers are always talking about their depressions (which in fact may trace to all the alcohol they drink and their uncertain livelihoods).

In any case, Andreasen concludes from her study that the families of writers were "riddled with both creativity and mental illness, while in the families of the control subjects, much of the illness and creativity seemed to be randomly scattered."

The sample was, alas, exceedingly small, although the differences between the writers and controls reached statistical significance. After centuries of speculation, however, scientific evidence finally exists that alcoholism, manic-depressive disease, and creativity may indeed be connected at a genetic level. More such studies are needed, but they are hard to do. Recall the *Writer's Digest* questionnaire, ignored or panned by almost all the subscribers. A touchy group, writers.

To summarize, alcoholic writers give the impression of being sad people who may or may not have clinical depressions related to their alcoholism. There appear to be genes for depression, genes for alcoholism, and genes for writing talent. Whether they are the *same* genes remains an open question, despite Andreasen's admirable study. Why alcoholic writers tend to be loners also remains unanswered, but a chronic depression must clearly be considered a possible factor, since depressives tend to be socially isolated.

Why America?

If alcoholism is a "disease of individualism," then America, the home of "rugged individualism," should have its share of it. Actually, there are probably no more alcoholics in America than in Scandinavia, Eastern Europe, Russia, France, and several other countries. But there do seem to be more alcoholic writers.

Maybe, again, "loner" is the link. Perhaps no country has canonized the loner like the Americans. As Robert Wilshire said, "The loner who is able to survive on his own cunning, intuition, and craft is held in esteem by Americans. The cowboy, the private eye, the rebel against society, all have been romanticized in fiction as well as fact." Jay Gatsby was a loner. Despite his need for human contact he remained aloof and independent.

With the aloofness is a certain sadness. (Shades of the Andreasen study!) According to Leon Edel, writers transform the sadness into art. He calls the "sadness of life" *tristimania*: It describes the component of depression in art, "for nothing is more chronic among writers than their sadness." In a story by Henry James, one of the characters, a writer, also connects sadness to art: "We live in the dark, we do what we can, the rest is the madness of art." The phrase "madness of art" appealed to Truman Capote, among other writers. In *Music for Chameleons* Capote wrote:

> Mr. James is laying it on the line there; he is telling the truth. In the darkest part of the truth, the maddest part of madness, is the relentless gambling involved! Writers, at least those who take genuine risk, who are willing to bite the bullet and walk the plank, have a lot in common with another breed of lonely men—the guys who make a living shooting pool and dealing cards.

Guys, in short, much admired by Americans.

As Wilshire points out, tristimania is similar to what Jellinek calls "vague spiritual longings" or the "vile melancholy" Dr. Johnson is said to have inherited from his father. "These feelings of sadness," Wilshire writes, "the alcoholic tries to drown in an ocean of liquor. The writer tries to exterminate them with words. The alcoholic writers do both—quite often at the expense of their writing." (Again, the depression link.)

As writers tend to view themselves as loners, so do alcoholics, at least in America. In *Twelve Steps and Twelve Traditions*, the handbook of Alcoholics Anonymous, written by Americans, the loner-alcoholic is pummeled without mercy:

> But it is from our twisted relations with family, friends, and society at large that many of us have suffered the most. We have been especially stupid and stubborn about them. *The primary fact that we fail to recognize is our total inability to form a true partnership*

with another human being. Our egomania digs two disastrous pit-falls. Either we insist upon dominating the people we know or we depend upon them far too much. If we lean too heavily on people, they will sooner or later fail us, for they are human too, and cannot possibly meet our incessant demands. In this way our insecurity grows and festers. When we habitually try to manipulate others to our own willful desires, they revolt, and resist us heavily. Then we develop hurt feelings, a sense of persecution, and a desire to retaliate. As we redouble our efforts at control, and continue to fail, our suffering becomes acute and constant. We have not once sought to be one in a family, to be a friend among friends, to be a worker among workers, to be a useful member of society. Always we tried to struggle to the top of the heap, or to hide underneath it. This self-centered behavior blocks a partnership relation with any one of those about us. Of true brotherhood we had small comprehension. [Italics added.]

Alcoholics Anonymous has helped many alcoholics but apparently not too many alcoholic writers. None of the eight writers in this book benefited from AA, if tried (Poe attended something like AA in the 1840s). Perhaps alcoholic writers reject AA on the same grounds they usually reject psychiatric treatment or psycho-analysis: it threatens their ability to write.

There are other reasons why America provided fertile ground for the epidemic. One is a curious ambivalence toward drinking often commented on by foreigners. As Alfred Kazin observed, America has always been a hard-drinking country despite the many places and times in which alcohol has been forbidden in law. He writes:

Even in Puritan days Americans were amazingly hard drinkers. It is history that liquor up to the Civil War was cheap as well as plentiful. In the first decades of the 19th century, spirits cost all of 25 cents a gallon domestic, and $1 imported. From 1818 to 1862 there were no taxes whatever on American whiskey, and it took the federal government's need of revenue during the Civil War to change things. The temperance movement, the Prohibitionist movement, the anti-Saloon League were all powerful church-supported bodies, but no more powerful than the "liquor inter-ests" and the freedom and ease that American males acquired for a 4-cents glass of beer in the saloon. America's entry into World War I and the need to conserve grain finally put Prohibition across in 1918. Whereupon the line was marked between what H.L. Mencken called the "Booboisie" and the party of sophistica-tion. In the 20s, drinking was the most accessible form of prestige for would-be sophisticates; and this continued to be the case within the professional and wealthy classes as the "tea party" of the 20s became the cocktail party of the 50s (a time when the clientele of Alcoholics Anonymous showed a more representative cross section of middle-class society than Congress).

In the 1920s, when the heavy drinking really began, Fitzgerald said that he and his generation "drank cocktails before meals like Americans, wines and brandies like Frenchmen, Scotch-and-soda like the English. This preposterous mélange was like a gigantic cocktail in a nightmare." Reading this, Georges Simenon would have said (in French, no doubt) "Amen!"

America's ambivalence toward drinking is expressed in humor and slang. As earlier noted, a quarter of the *New Yorker* cartoons show somebody drinking and one-sixth show somebody drunk. After sex, drunkenness is the most popular topic for humorous greeting cards. Edmund Wilson once listed over one hundred words for drunkenness used in the United States during Prohibi-tion, arranged in order of the degree of intensity, beginning with *lit* and *oiled* and ending with *jingles* and *burn with a low blue flame*. Ben-jamin Franklin listed over two hundred!

The notion of "moderate" drinking seems to be rather recent in America. Frontier saloons were places to get drunk, not "have a beer." Speakeasies were places to get drunk. Fraternity parties, well into the present era, were occasions to get drunk (and perhaps still are).

Of those who got "lit" now and then, most survived and either stopped drinking or drank less as they got older. But there were victims, many victims, many of them writers. The boozy fellowship led to binges, then remorse and a vow to stop or cut down. Jack London recalled how it was in *John Barleycorn:*

Never again would I get drunk. All I wanted, and all I would take, was just enough to glow and warm me, to kick geniality alive in me and put laughter in my throat and stir the maggots of imagination slightly in my brain. Oh, I was thoroughly master of myself, and of John Barleycorn.

But London was an American alcoholic and, as mentioned in the Simenon chapter, American alcoholics can abstain from alcohol but not moderate. Vowing to limit himself to one cocktail a day, London found that

the same stimulus to the human organism will not continue to produce the same response. By and by I discovered there was no kick at all in one cocktail. One cocktail left me dead. There was no glow, no laughter, no tickle. Two or three cocktails were required to produce the original effect of one. And I wanted that effect. I drank my first cocktail at eleven-thirty when I took the morning's mail into the hammock, and I drank my second cocktail an hour later just before I ate. I got into the habit of crawling out of the hammock ten minutes earlier so as to find time and decency for two more cocktails ere I ate. This became schedule—three cocktails in the hour that intervened between my desk and dinner. And these were two of the deadliest drinking habits: regular drinking and solitary drinking. I was always willing to drink when anyone was around. I drank by myself when no one was around.

Simenon said he learned to become ashamed of his drinking in America; he had never been ashamed of his drinking in France. America's Puritan tradition could never be reconciled with the American's thirst.

"There are periods and occasions when drinking is in the air, even seems to be a moral necessity," Kazin wrote. One reason it was "in the air" in the twenties was the great changeover from the Old World and small-town America to city living, big money, and the big time. With this came decadence.

The English writer Dan Davin says the "decadence which was the culmination of romanticism in Europe at the turn of the century . . . lingered on or came late to America, and the self-destructiveness typical of decadence—and the destruction of form itself in the pursuit of originality—has been reinforced by the characteristic American vigor, translating genius as an infinite capacity for taking pain and being thirstiest with the mostest, with the result that the consequent dissolution is so much more cataclysmic and picturesque than, say, the anemic decline of an Ernest Dowson."

Most Americans have never heard of Ernest Dowson, perhaps because his decline was so anemic.

A more prosaic explanation for some of the alcoholic American writers was their origin as newspapermen in an age when heavy drinking was part of the job description of a reporter. (Half or more of the well-known alcoholic writers in the first half of the century at one time worked for newspapers or magazines.)

Jim Bishop recalled that some years ago there were fifteen "healthy newspapers in New York"—each with a saloon beside it. The drinkery was more than an atmosphere of surcease; it was a place where reporters, photographers, engravers, printers, and editors had credit ratings.

> Those who imbibed used what I presume is an incontrovertible defense: the daily tensions of news-gathering, of trying to get the whole story and get it in time for the aptly named "deadline"; to wait to read competitive newspapers to learn if they had an integral part of the story which we missed; the frustration of researching a good yarn all the way into the ground and then have the City Editor hold up two fingers pinched together, murmuring: "Give me three graphs," cause many good men to be tightly wound, like cheap alarm clocks set to ring at the whim of the city desk. Many left the office for the saloon next door, intending to have two before hopping the commuter train. However, the bar conversation was always so rich and revealing, the joy of jawing among one's confreres often led to one more, and one more, and one more.
>
> *The major cause of drinking is the human hangover.* [An astute observation, with scientific evidence to back it.] Many good journalists found it impossible to think with any degree of reliability the next morning after confessing all to a bottle. Thus drink led to

hangover; hangover led to drink and yet, in retrospect, I suggest that there were fewer alcoholics in the editorial department than on the average police department. As a class in a classless society, the retired rich are the worst.

Police departments and the retired rich haven't been studied, but their fund of good-old-drinking-crony stories will never match the newspaperman's. At a National Council on Alcoholism forum on drinking writers, the Front Page tradition was much discussed. Roger Kahn thought sports reporters were in particular danger. One reason was that people who ran American sports were always giving sportswriters free drinks. "It was a way of controlling, manipulating, influencing media people . . . in the press room the food is poor and the booze good. The victims it cultivates are alcohol-dependent persons." Continuing:

> The tradition of sports journalism provides that if the alcohol-dependent reporter, or the alcoholic, is late to a game, somebody else fills in for him. Somebody else writes his story. That way there is a free permissiveness. You certainly can get drunk and miss the game on Thursday; somebody else will fill you in, the person will write for you. The person who doesn't, who doesn't write for an alcoholic, is scorned by the other writers.
>
> There is the story of the late Arch Murray, who drank more than any other sports writer I had encountered, who got to a double-header about the seventh inning of the second game and said, "Fill me in"—which, essentially, meant tell me how all the outs were made up until this point. So some Samaritan started to fill him in, starting with the first inning of the first game. In the third inning of the second game, he said, "There was a line drive to left field and the left fielder ran back and made one hell of a catch"— and Arch Murray said: "I'll be the judge of that."

Heavy drinking was socially acceptable in journalism, "certainly in an earlier generation before there was so much pot," continued Kahn. "It was a way of being macho but I think the tendency [to drink a lot] had to be there first." Ring Lardner, Jr., agreed. Heavy drinking was common on New York newspapers in the thirties when he became a reporter and was probably even greater in his father's day, he said.

Certainly on the *Chicago Tribune* when Ben Hecht and Charles

MacArthur were young reporters . . . the saloon was an adjunct to the newspaper office . . . you went from the office to the bar. Hours may have had something to do with it. The newspaperman would work on different kinds of shifts and, you know, you'd start at ten in the morning and work sort of a normal day, or you would start working at six and finish working at two in the morning, at which time a person didn't feel like going home and there wasn't much else to do but go to what bars were still open.

In even earlier days, newspapermen, like short-order cooks, were itinerants. As one forum discussant said, "If a newspaperman got drunk and screwed himself up in one town, he could hop to another city where, as a newspaperman with a track record, he could fall into another job." Newspapermen were often alcoholic, he believed, because they could always move on to new jobs.

The writers at the forum concluded that journalists as well as novelists have a tendency to mythologize and romanticize alcoholism, which, in truth, is a "down-dirty seedy disease" and nowadays can be overcome. They agree there is less drinking among reporters today than in the past. Maybe this is one reason the great American epidemic of alcoholic writers seems to be easing.

Hemingway had a theory explaining why so many American writers became alcoholic. It was because they had mixed feelings about their craft: they wanted to be great writers who would be remembered forever but also rich and famous writers. They didn't want to wàit for posterity to judge them; they wanted to be successful right now.

This put a lot of strain on them. It was America's fault. William James had called success a "bitch goddess" and said it was the great American deity. Hemingway agreed. He called alcohol the "Giant Killer," the giant being America with its worship of success. Alfred Kazin, who seems to like the Hemingway theory, elaborates:

The history of American writers starting as early as the nineteenth century has been marked by unnatural strain, physical isolation, an alienation from the supposedly sweet and lovely aspects of American life. Poe, a writer and editor of genius, was always desperate for money . . . and helped to sell the marketplace psychology among American writers. When that idea became rampant, as in the 1920s, the big money and big time began to seem possible for serious writers. That's when the really big writing drinkers emerged.

This is the stress theory of alcoholism, rejected by most authorities on alcoholism. Viewing the epidemic from across the Atlantic, however, Dan Davin saw evidence for Hemingway's theory in Hemingway's letters. They are full, he says, of

explicit desire to become "the champ" and talk of going twenty rounds (in the ring rather than the bar), with Tolstoy. Can it be there is some confusion in the minds of some American writers between success and the art, and success in terms of royalties and public acclaim; and that the stress caused by this competitiveness compels an increasing and undue resort to alcohol? Or is it a vestige of frontier machismo: that even a writer must show that he is a weakling neither in life nor in letters?

Or, Davin asks, was it the strong whiskey served in American bars?

He was speculating like the rest of us.

The Price

Maybe Homer was a drinker. He was blind, but then Thurber was blind and he was a drinker. Homer does dwell on wine—the "red-wine sea," etc. There is no reliable Homer biography, so how shall we know?

Before Homer, the cave painters had been drinkers. Or at least that's the opinion of a historian of wine who felt cave painters of "such undoubted intelligence must be assumed to be familiar with the inspirational essence of wine":

We may be able, at least in argument, to push the original date of wine-making back to the distant age of the Magdalenian rock-painters, 10,000 years ago or more . . . a prehistoric vine *Vitis silvestris* is more or less resistant to frost and . . . even in the somewhat cold climate of the Magdalenian period this vine may have been able to ripen its grapes; and if it could do so, then the rock-painters may well have drunk wine. . . . When we consider the skill of the Magdalenian rock paintings it is hard to believe that men who exploited such an art did not also exploit the accidental discovery of wine.

The need for something like alcohol is certainly as old as man, *Homo anxius*. According to Berton Roueché:

The basic needs of the human race, its members have long agreed, are food, clothing, and shelter. To that fundamental trinity most modern authorities would add, as equally compelling, security and love. There are, however, many other needs whose satisfaction, though somewhat less essential, can seldom be comfortably denied. One of these, and perhaps the most insistent, is an occasional release from the intolerable clutch of reality. All men throughout recorded history have known this tyranny of memory and mind, and all have sought, and invariably found, some reliable means of briefly loosening its grip.

But for many American writers during this century the loosening has been costly. In her lovely memoir about her father, Susan Cheever says that for years her father had been "proud of his ability to imbibe large amounts of hard liquor . . . drinking was a manly indulgence, a confirmation of power and courage and masculine endurance. *All great writers drank*" (italics added).

Then she quotes a passage from his journals, written in 1969, when he was suffering greatly from debt and alcohol, a passage so lyrically painful it will serve to end these sad meditations:

My incantation has changed. I am no longer sitting under an apple tree in clean chinos reading. I am sitting naked in the yellow chair in the dining room. In my hand there is a large crystal glass filled to the brim with honey colored whiskey. There are two ice cubes in the whiskey. I am smoking six or seven cigarettes and thinking contentedly about my interesting travels in Egypt and Russia. When the glass is empty I fill it again with ice and whiskey and light another cigarette although there are several burning in the ashtray. I am sitting naked in a yellow chair drinking whiskey and smoking six or seven cigarettes.